T0283566

Mama

Mama

A Queer Black Woman's Story
of a Family Lost and Found

Nikkya Hargrove

ALGONQUIN BOOKS
OF CHAPEL HILL
2024

Published by
ALGONQUIN BOOKS OF CHAPEL HILL
an imprint of Workman Publishing
a division of Hachette Book Group, Inc.
1290 Avenue of the Americas
New York, NY 10104

The Algonquin Books of Chapel Hill name and logo are registered
trademarks of Hachette Book Group, Inc.

Printed in the United States of America.
Design by Steve Godwin.

This book is memoir and reflects the author's present recollections of
experiences over time. Some names and characteristics have been
changed, and some dialogue has been re-created.

The publisher is not responsible for websites (or their content)
that are not owned by the publisher.

Library of Congress Cataloging-in-Publication Data
Names: Hargrove, Nikkya, [date]– author.
Title: Mama : a queer Black woman's story of a family lost
and found / Nikkya Hargrove.
Description: First edition. | New York, NY : Algonquin Books of
Chapel Hill, [2024] | Identifiers: LCCN 2024027921 (print) |
LCCN 2024027922 (ebook) |
ISBN 9781643751580 (hardcover) | ISBN 9781643756172 (ebook)
Subjects: LCSH: Hargrove, Nikkya, [date]– | Mothers—United States—
Biography. | Lesbian mothers—United States—Biography. | African American
mothers—United States—Biography. | African American lesbians—United
States—Biography. | Imprisonment—Moral and ethical aspects—United
States. | Foster home care—Moral and ethical aspects—United States. |
Generational trauma—United States. | African American families—Effect of
imprisonment on. | Prisoners' families—Effect of imprisonment on—United States.
Classification: LCC HQ75.53 .H368 2024 (print) | LCC HQ75.53 (ebook) |
DDC 306.874/3086640973—dc23/eng/20240702
LC record available at https://lccn.loc.gov/2024027921
LC ebook record available at https://lccn.loc.gov/2024027922

10 9 8 7 6 5 4 3 2 1
First Edition

For Jonathan

Mama

Prologue

THEY SEARCH EVERY crevice of my mother's soft, brown body. The rolls at her waistline, proof she carried four babies, must be checked. A female guard inspects under each bulge, her light-blue eyes and rough white hands moving over every inch. My mother's breasts, their weight known for giving her back pain, are lifted one by one.

I won't learn this until much later, but my mother is probed for weapons, the kind inmates make and take into visiting rooms with the purpose of hurting someone. A toothbrush shaved down to a pointed tip, at the ready to stab another inmate. This is just one of the things the guards searched my mother's body for.

The flesh of her buttocks and the lips of her vagina are inspected, because that's where inmates hide latex gloves filled with drugs. There are no drugs to be found inside my mother's body, no balloons filled with anything. No crack cocaine or any other type of drug is tucked inside.

Only after her body has been deemed safe is she allowed to

enter the visiting room. "Clean and cleared" are the words she needs to hear before she is allowed to see her family: her daughter, her mother, her father.

My mother waits behind a black steel door in the company of two guards, standing in silence until the sound of the buzzer lets me into the visiting room. I am already feeling ashamed—for her, for me, for all of us.

I am fourteen years old.

Finally, my mother enters, her round cheeks plump from her smile. Her honey-blond bob frames her round face, and a small dimple and dark-red lipstick make her appear cheerier than I assume she is. She greets us with an "Oh, I am so glad you came!" She answers questions with short, quick responses: "Good!" "Fine." "No." "How come?"

It baffles me how she can enter every visiting room with that smile. Stripped of her dignity, she does not share the pain she must feel, the embarrassment, the reality of her situation. I imagine it's because we, her family, already have enough to deal with because of her mistakes. Or perhaps, after so much time living in this jail, my mother is numb to her emotions.

She cannot greet me with a hug or touch my shoulder. Nothing can be handed from my mother to us. And anything we want to give her—clothes, noncommissary food, soap, even letters—needs to be sent directly to the jail to be inspected, in advance of or after our visit. I know if I were in her shoes, I would cry every single time. I would walk through the heavy doors, wanting to hold my mom or dad or daughter, and whisper how sorry I am, how raw and hurt I feel after a stranger looked into my most private parts. But I am not my mother, and for this I am grateful.

Like my mother, though, during those visits, I never let the tears fall that would confirm my sadness. I never show my mother anything at all. I keep my feelings inside, under lock and key. We are all casualties of the war on drugs. We bear the toll of the life she's chosen.

So we keep the conversation light. We do not go deep. We do not ask about fears, wants, or needs. We update her on family members; we talk about friends she has inside. The details my mother shares paint portraits of the other people in her life: her cellmates, mostly Black or brown women who have sold their bodies for drugs, murdered an abusive lover, or became so lost in a relationship with a man that somehow robbery seemed okay. She tells us about the guards who question why she is in jail again, the boyfriend who doesn't visit, the young girls she voluntarily mentors.

I don't ask her any questions. Instead, I imagine my mother behind bars: She wears an orange jumpsuit, her fingers wrapped tightly around the steel poles as the orange hue of the setting sun casts a shadow on the reality that she's stuck there. She looks left and then right, waiting for a guard to walk by, just to have someone to talk to, before she lowers her head when she realizes that no one is coming.

IT IS NOT until years later that she offered me this: "The cell was small, and those girls got on my nerves. It took everything I had not to fight them. The cell had a bathroom in it. And the smell, the smell of piss, all of the time in jail! I made some good friends while I was there, but it was definitely a lonely place."

I would never hear about the altercations or the abuse she faced. Denial and silence was the name of the game, and perhaps the only way she knew how to protect me. Over the years, a few stories about my birth and my childhood have been passed down to me. Aunts and uncles told me, *Your mother hung out on the streets. Your mother was beaten up and bloodied after a fight with a boyfriend, and I washed her body off in the bathtub.* The stories I've heard have holes in them, incomplete either because my aunts and uncles do not remember the truth or because the truth is too hard for them to handle.

In my infrequent letters, I eventually found the courage to ask my mother the questions I was too scared to ask during those visits while in the company of my grandparents: Why did she choose drugs over me? Why did jail appeal to her so? Why wasn't I enough? In my neat handwriting, I shared with her my own stories—about living with Nanny and Poppy on Long Island, my Honors English class, my cousin and my friends, the high school dramas of my life. I shared and reshared my excitement about getting my driver's license and a job, hoping to one day afford to pay for my dream car—a Honda Civic with a CD player.

In her letters back to me, she called me by her nickname for me—Mama—and she told me how beautiful my handwriting was: *Just like mine.* I prayed it was the only trait we shared. She told me how much she missed home and her own mother. She told me how much she missed me. I never believed her, because she never found her way back to me when she was free.

I know now that my letters would reach her opened, already read by the guards. What were they looking for? Did they laugh at my childish stories? Did they presume I, too, would end up in jail? Did they even think about me at all?

I've never been in jail, but I imagine the isolation I felt growing up feels something like being locked in a small cell: No one to depend on but yourself. No one around to call Mama.

ONE DAY, THOUGH, I'd become somebody's mama. I'd struggle in ways my mother never had, carrying the constant worries that perhaps only a parent who is truly present brings. Now, I hold the birth stories of my own kids forever etched in my heart. I write down the details they may one day want to know, just like I wanted to know mine.

Being a mother requires so much emotional, physical, and spiritual strength. It can be exhausting, but as parents—good parents—we make the decision to be better people. We choose to put our children ahead of our own dreams and desires, reassured by the belief that one day we will be able to hold both our dreams and parenthood in the same space.

When I became somebody's mama, I was forced to look at myself more honestly, more bravely, allowing the pain that defined my past to wash over me, baptizing me, so I could forge a life I love for my kids and me. I came to realize that being a parent was my calling.

I know now that being called Mama is a privilege—and a gift worth unpacking.

PART ONE

1

———

WHILE I MADE the eight-hour drive from Virginia, I tapped the worn black steering wheel, trying to soothe my fears of the unknown. In a Long Island hospital miles away, cocaine ran through the veins of my newborn baby brother. I tested my memory by trying to name a song on the radio, distracting myself from what I was heading toward.

What would my relationship with him be like? Would he feel like my half brother?

With each twist and turn, I heard small pebbles lift from the pavement, catch in my tires, and spit back out. Barren trees lined the road, each quickly flashing out of view.

The flatness of the Long Island Expressway, a road I had driven thousands of times before, felt different today. A heaviness filled my chest, and I recognized it as anxiety. My car, a gray Volkswagen Passat wagon, barreled down the road at an uncomfortable pace—sixty, sixty-five, seventy. My worry ticked up with the orange dial on my speedometer.

Was my brother healthy? Did he have his ten fingers and ten toes? Was he going through withdrawal? Had anyone held him yet?

All I knew was that my mother's baby had been born, and that in the state of New York when a newborn's toxicology report tests positive for drugs, Child Protective Services gets called in immediately. *He may have to go to foster care,* I told myself, trying to prepare for every scenario, unsure if he would become yet another baby for my grandparents to raise, forcing them to live in some in-between land of grandparent and parent. But I also harbored an alternative solution.

And then I had another thought: *My mother may die. Her heart just might give out this time.*

How could I prepare myself for that?

My baby brother had been born early, expected Christmas 2006 but instead arriving soon after Thanksgiving. Two nights before his birth, my mother smoked a cocktail of drugs. Crack cocaine had long been her drug of choice, but this time it was laced with something else—what exactly, she didn't know. She loved crack cocaine almost as much as she loved her four children—maybe even more.

This time, her excuse for using was the need to release pent-up tension from an argument she'd had with my aunt Lady, her older sister. Aunt Lady had a raspy voice from years of smoking Newport 100s. I remember watching her hands as she unwrapped the cellophane on a new pack of cigarettes. When she talked, her cigarette would move up and down quickly with every word she spoke. I never understood why cigarette smoking appealed to her so much until one day I heard her having a conversation with my mom. "When you have a good cup of coffee and that first cigarette of the morning, what a high it is," she said.

Over the years, her lips and hands darkened from the nicotine, one shade darker than her original, light-brown skin color. Her coarse dark-brown hair was usually styled in a short bob, warranting the use of a silk scarf while she slept. When she spoke to me, there was a crassness in her tone. I never knew, and still really don't know, if what she resented was my very existence. Maybe she allowed her anger toward my mother to color how she spoke to me. Or it could be that she wished her mother—my grandmother—would treat *her* like she treated me, as if I were her own daughter.

For half of high school, I lived in Lady's house, feeling like I was Cinderella before she met the prince. My grandparents, with whom I'd spent most of my life till then, had decided to move back to Virginia and eventually live out their retirement years there. I'd wanted to finish high school in New York. My grandfather was still looking for work, so he, too, needed to stay on Long Island for a while. Nanny and my little sister, Ciara, rented a condo in Virginia, and Poppy continued working for Tropicana, making deliveries to different delis and even a jail my mother once spent time in. For two years, he and I shared a small room with a white metal-framed bunk bed at Aunt Lady's, until he found a new job and I graduated.

Most often, Poppy would cook dinner for everyone, which included Lady's husband, Bob, and their daughter, Natasha, and their son, Robert, who we called Manny. The expectation was

that the three kids would do the dishes and clean the house—
the hope was to instill in us the understanding that running a
household required the cooperation of all family members—but
it ended being mostly me doing the cleaning up. And there was
a lot of it.

My mother and Lady loved each other but didn't know how
to show it. For as long as I can remember, they expressed their
love through conflict. They were experts at arguing, their voices
growing higher and higher as each quarrel escalated. Two nights
before my brother was born, Aunt Lady and my mother had
tried desperately to make their points, digging up old wrongdo-
ings, wounds that should have stayed buried or been dealt with
long before in healthier ways. After the fight, my mother called,
asking to stay with me.

MY AUNT'S REAL name was Wanda, but she'd picked up the nickname Lady as a child because of the way she handled her siblings
and how she spoke to adults, moving through the world with a
kind of confidence and assertiveness well beyond her age. My
mother and Lady were two of the six children my grandmother
had with her first husband, Thomas, and they experienced life
with a father who preferred the bottle to being a parent.

My mother, Aunt Lady, and Uncle Wayne were the oldest,
then came Uncle Main, Aunt Kendra, and finally the baby, Aunt
She-She. They were all accustomed to their father's anger, but
one explosive argument in particular stood out: It was raining
when his weekly poker game was interrupted by wet tire tracks.

Wayne had rolled his bike across the kitchen's linoleum floor as he steered it toward the basement to store it.

The trauma still runs hot whenever any of the siblings tell the story, sometimes laughing off the seriousness of what happened but always with an acknowledgment that their lives were changed forever. Thomas yelled at Wayne, then a scrawny fifteen-year-old, "Get dat wet bike outta my house." Then Thomas punched Wayne in the eye. Wayne took the bike back outside, rode it to the party his mother was at, and told her what his father had done. She stuffed his bike into her trunk, and they drove back home to confront Thomas.

"You don't hit him over a bike," she told her husband.

In answer, Thomas hit her.

When his hand collided with her face, all six children ran and jumped on top of him. The three oldest kids tackled his upper body while the three younger kids grabbed on to his legs and ankles, clawing and biting their way to save their mother.

Once Thomas was on the ground, my grandmother packed up what belongings she could, and then she grabbed the kids and they all ran outside and piled into her Chevy, its engine still hot, the bike still in the trunk. The rain was still pouring down, and in the race to leave, Nanny backed over Pam, their family dog, a stray they'd taken in. She didn't stop—she had herself and her kids to save from the hands of her husband.

"That wasn't the first fuckin' time he hit her," Uncle Main said when he recently told me this story again. "That was just the time we said we weren't fuckin' dealing with it anymore."

What I know about the miseries my aunts and uncles endured as children, the ones they told me about and the ones they didn't feel comfortable disclosing, is that they followed them into adulthood—through addiction, dropping out of high school, unhappy marriages, and questionable parental choices. Uncle Wayne started drinking at the age of nine and has held a Budweiser or a Heineken or a Colt 45—it doesn't matter what kind of beer, as long as he has one—in his hand for the last fifty-six years, though thank goodness he never turned abusive like his father. For my mother and Lady, partying and drugs became their go-to distraction. Aunt Lady would eventually learn to curb it. My mother, not so much.

To cope in healthy ways requires living, breathing examples of how to do it, and it takes practice. Broken people cannot fix other broken people, but those same people can pass down trauma without even knowing it, from one generation to the next.

WAS THE BABY in the neonatal intensive care unit? Would he have a severe disability?

As angry as I was at my mother as I sped toward the hospital, I also understood her frustration, her desire to find comfort in drugs after her argument with Lady. What she really wanted was relief from her situation, from the life she found herself in, a life she must have blamed herself for. I imagined her with her big belly resting between her legs, her full lips wrapped around the opening of a crack pipe as she crouched low, fearful of who might find her. That smoke was her escape—and the fog that kept her living in the land of denial and regret.

After she smoked, her uterus had ruptured, labor began, and an emergency C-section was needed. Now she was in the ICU, her life hanging in the balance, along with the life of the baby who had been inside her.

I glanced at my silver flip phone on the passenger seat and decided that I would try calling the hospital again. I pushed REDIAL. "I'm checking on Lisa Eleazer and her baby," I said with an assertiveness I didn't really feel but thought of as a mother's tone. I was assuming the role of my mother's mama. It was a role I was intimately familiar with, since my own mother called me Mama, a label that branded me as someone she thought would love her unconditionally. "Are they okay?"

"Yes," the nurse said. "And that's all I can say."

She hung up without saying goodbye.

I was being shut out before I'd even arrived. I still knew nothing more than that my baby brother was in the care of Child Protective Services. Our mother's neglect meant he was in a tangled system I was already skeptical of. My hands began to sweat. I was some forty miles from my exit. I applied more pressure to the gas pedal.

I could not let fear get a hold of me now.

AT TWENTY-FOUR, I'D created a life for myself without any help from my mother, and her neediness did not fit easily into that life. She was really good at showing up when it was convenient for her but not for me. The constant calls and requests for help were a burden, but I loved her no matter how broken she was. We definitely had a mother-daughter relationship; it's just that our roles were reversed.

After I graduated from Bard College in 2005 with a degree in human rights, my first job was working as a case manager for mentally ill adolescents at a nonprofit in upstate New York. I lived with my girlfriend, Kate, in a small rural town in the Hudson Valley, not far from Woodstock.

It was during that time that my mom called asking for her biggest favor yet.

Kate and I shared a sunny, spacious one-bedroom apartment with our dogs, Bella and Bailey. Bella, a brown-and-white cocker spaniel, was spoiled and easygoing, while Bailey, our large Weimaraner, was goofy and gentle. Both taught me about responsibility and commitment, maybe more so than my relationship with Kate did.

I was Kate's first serious girlfriend. We met in my senior year of college. She'd graduated the year before me from another college, as a pre-med major. We were immediately attracted to each other. I remember staring into her light-blue eyes our entire first date, her straight blond hair brushing against my face during what I assumed would be just a hookup. It quickly turned into more. I was smitten.

Kate shared stories about her absent father that I identified with, but also about a mother and stepfather who cared for her in ways my mother hadn't. Her white skin gave her a privilege I would never know. It seemed to me that her blond hair and blue eyes also made it easier for her to get what she wanted. I was the one with a complicated childhood. I was the one with a mother who had a drug addiction and who never finished high school. I was the one who had to hope and pray not to be like my mother. I loved Kate because she represented everything I wasn't.

Kate introduced me to the Wattamelon Roll. When she mentioned it to me one night at the kitchen sink when we were cleaning up after dinner, she said it as if she'd told me the same thing a thousand times before: "Man, I want Wattamelon Roll cake."

I turned my head and said, "Kate, I've never seen a watermelon roll cake . . . anywhere, ever." And we both laughed.

She went on washing the dishes, the white suds disappearing underneath the water with each movement she made. I stood next to her, drying the plates, forks, and cups with a dish towel, as she explained to me what a Wattamelon Roll was.

"Didn't you ever have one at Friendly's?" she asked me, as if *she'd* heard *me* talk about my family's Friday night trips to Friendly's. She had not. We didn't go to Friendly's. Maybe once, but it certainly wasn't a regular occurrence. "I used to go all of the time with my mom," Kate continued. "And then we saw the ice cream. It's ice cream made to look like a real watermelon, but it's not. It's, like, ice cream in the shape of a watermelon. Well, not *ice cream* ice cream, but sherbet. Let's get some so you can try it," she said. And she found it at our local ShopRite.

I loved sharing the holiday season with Kate, though I had never known the kind of bliss she felt about Christmas. Kate started playing Christmas music the day after Thanksgiving. It was Kate who taught me how special a gift of homemade

Christmas cookies could be. One year, we decided to bake dozens of different cookie recipes together. "Baking is about getting messy, and just having fun," she told me. "And, of course, when it's done, you can eat as many delicious cookies as you'd like." There was a kind of magic in her bright blue eyes that was alive and well from the first snowfall to the dropping of the ball in Times Square.

Living through all the holidays with Kate meant I got to truly see how someone could be an adult and still access the child inside. Kate did that. It wasn't about the gift giving but about the experiences and the memories. And though I didn't have joyful holiday memories from my childhood that included my mother in them, she brought me the experiences so I could make new memories.

I WAS THE one who proposed to Kate. I wanted stability. I wanted to create the kind of family I imagined Kate had. She smiled through the entirety of her phone calls with her mother and celebrated each time a care package from her arrived. I could choose partners better than my mother had. I felt it was time.

Before I proposed, we'd talked about when we would get married. One day, the two of us decided to go to Zales jewelry store to check out what kind of engagement rings we might like. I have a tendency to be impulsive, so during my next trip to the mall, I bought the emerald-cut ring Kate liked with my newly opened Zales credit card. I held on to the dark-maroon box for a while, with an idea of how I wanted to propose but no real plan. Instead, one evening, I walked her into our living room and asked her to sit on the couch. I felt a bit of trepidation. I had the odd sense that it was the wrong decision, but I was still elated when she said yes.

I knew getting from that yes to walking down the aisle would be a battle. We had much to overcome and reconcile as a couple but also as individuals. She needed to come to terms with her sexuality—I was only the second woman she'd been with—and her mother, with whom she was ostensibly so close and to whom she told almost everything, didn't know we were involved, let alone how much we meant to each other. Kate simply wasn't ready to declare whether she identified as a bisexual person, a queer person, a lesbian, or some version of all three. She didn't tell her mother about our engagement even after she said yes.

I had my issues, too. I needed to figure out how to manage my own family, especially my mother. I needed to learn how and when to open up to Kate, to lean into the fact that this was someone who I was going to spend my life with. I needed to not be afraid she'd leave me when things got hard.

Then there were our careers, which neither of us had quite figured out. She originally wanted to be a doctor, but now she wasn't so sure. I had also thought of becoming a doctor—a pediatrician or an ob-gyn. Growing up, I'd spent many hours daydreaming about delivering babies or caring for sick kids. Now, I was considering going to graduate school to become a psychologist, but I didn't want to take out more student loans.

We went about our lives as an engaged couple, regardless. I hoped our love for each other would be strong enough to shelter us when storms threatened to sweep us away.

Maybe I was blinded by how in tune our bodies were. Maybe I was too optimistic, thinking she would recognize that her love for me was more important than her fear of committing to being with a woman, and that she would fight for what she wanted.

But maybe I just wasn't a priority for her—just like I wasn't for my mother.

ONE DAY, WHILE Kate and I sat in our living room, my mother called unexpectedly. At the time, she was pregnant and living with Lady. Aunt Lady had risen through the ranks working for the Internal Revenue Service, and she now managed teams and got to tell people what to do.

Lady's husband, Bob, showed up for me as much as he showed up for his own kids. He was the one who made sure there was a hearty snack at the ready for us when we'd come after a long day in high school. He was the one who encouraged me to try a new sport. He was the one who listened to me whenever I needed to vent about my mother. He was in my life even after he and Lady got divorced in 2008.

As for Lady, she was the family's repairer. She would patch up problems, including the catastrophic ones caused by my mother. Her siblings would turn to her when they didn't have a place to live or were in sticky legal situations, and she'd coach them through it. Most of my aunts and uncles were still bouncing around Long Island, where they'd grown up and never left. I suppose they found comfort in staying close to home. Whether they lived in Mastic or Riverhead or Southampton, the North Shore was their true north, where they played out whatever dreams they had. And Lady was the one they called if their dreams turned into nightmares.

When my mother got deep into selling drugs or when she needed an address to use in order to be released from jail, Lady would be there. She was there when another of my mother's babies needed a home base in order to stay out of foster care or when a relative needed refuge after a bad breakup. She was there even after the police raided her house, with her own children inside, while they were looking for my mother.

Lady didn't always have it right—the right answers or the right way of doing things—but she showed up, giving of herself in ways no one else in my family seemed to have the fortitude to do. She was always ready to speak her mind, to quash an argument, or to push her own point to the bitter end, the smell of cigarettes on her breath accompanying each sentence that left her mouth. But when something was wrong, we called Lady.

Over the years, she became understandably worn-out by all the neediness. I didn't know it then, but her inclination to always say yes when family called on her was my first inkling of why saying no mattered so much to me.

Lady had inherited the house on Randall Street in Riverhead, payment for taking care of her father, Thomas, when he fell ill. It was the same house where Nanny, along with the kids, left Thomas after he hit her that rainy night many years before. After his death, Lady moved her own family into the house. Like so many times before, Lady had agreed to give this address to my mother's parole officer, who would check in and make sure my mother made it in before her 9 p.m. curfew.

In August of 2006, the sisters got into an argument, which ended with my mother stomping out and vowing never to return. In a last-ditch attempt to stay clean and do right by her then unborn baby, she called me.

"I have no place to go, Mama," my mother said. I braced myself for the inevitable. "Can I come stay with you?"

I took a deep breath in and held it.

"Let me talk to Kate about it. I'll call you back," I promised, even though I was unsure if I meant it.

I didn't have time to fully digest her request before my phone rang again. I looked down and saw my grandmother's number light up on the screen of my silver flip phone. I stared out the window at the woods beyond our apartment and took another deep breath. I answered.

"Nikki, have you spoken to your mom?"

"Yes. She asked if she could move in with us."

"She has nowhere to go. She's living in a car out in Riverhead," she said.

"Nan, I don't live here alone. I need to talk to Kate."

My tone surprised me. I'd never spoken to my grandmother with such assertiveness, but I was tired of bailing my mother out—whether it was out of jail or something else. I did not want to play the same role as Lady, didn't have the same life experience or desire to clean up other people's messes. Of course, I knew that allowing my forty-one-year-old pregnant mother to move in with us would stress Kate and our young relationship. But this was my mother, and I knew I could give her a safe place to stay, food to eat, and stability for the baby she was carrying.

I rehearsed the discussion I planned to have with Kate. It was much easier to get the words out in the imaginary exchange in my head:

You know, she's my mom, and I love her.

I could not live with myself if something happened to her or the baby while she's living in a car, knowing I could have helped her.

She needs a place to stay. What do you think about us helping her for a few weeks?

I knew it would be a hard conversation, but Kate's reaction when I actually asked, proved how fragile our relationship really was.

"No way," she said. "She's a drug addict who will probably steal from us. And on top of that, she's pregnant. No."

Kate wasn't entirely wrong to feel this way, but still her words stung. My bond with my mother was hard for any outsider to understand. It was clear that Kate would never have empathy for a poor, traumatized, uneducated Black woman with a substance-abuse problem. Kate existed in a world with less discrimination. She'd had a childhood filled with love and without jail or prison visits. Kate's mother had provided for her and didn't ask for help.

The truth is, though, that Kate's response gave me a way out, an escape from taking responsibility for how I really felt about my mother moving in with us.

When I called my mother back later that afternoon, I felt sick to my stomach.

"Hi, Mom."

"Hi, Mama," she said.

"I want you to move in, but you just can't. We have two dogs and a one-floor apartment, and we would hear you snoring through the wall. I'm sorry."

My words didn't make sense to me even as I said them. I was full of shit, and she knew it.

"Okay. I'll figure something out."

I heard the defeat in her voice, a feeling she knew all too well.

My mother would have to turn to plan B: moving back in with Lady. I feared their strained relationship would crumble further under the weight of my mother's issues. But if she had moved in with Kate and me, I would have lost myself in caring for her. My life would have revolved around making sure my mother had what she needed—just like it had so many times before. It would give my mother control over me in a way that I was no longer willing to cede.

Still, it felt like I had deserted her. I sat on my couch, looking through the window decorated by the canine-nose-print decals, and inhaled deeply. It was one thing to parent two dogs and something entirely different to be wholly responsible for another human being.

2

____

ON NOVEMBER 28, 2006, at 4:56 p.m., my baby brother was born.

The next day, I arrived at Riverhead's Peconic Bay Medical Center, a hospital in the same town where my mother grew up. It was a small, newly renovated facility, with an emergency room kept busy with drug overdoses and shootings. Alone, I rode the elevator up to the third floor with an empty feeling inside, prematurely exhausted by the conversation I was about to have with my mother.

When I found her room, she glanced at me, and as if we'd never skipped a beat, I was back visiting her in the most unsavory of situations. She gave me a tired hello, her smile halfhearted, her voice raspy from the breathing tube they'd taken out a few hours ago. I could smell dried blood as soon as I walked in, a telltale sign that she'd recently given birth. My mother's disappointment in herself, her situation, showed all over her face. I tried searching her eyes for answers, for some piece of the truth, but she avoided looking at me directly.

I know you didn't mean to relapse, I wanted to say. *And I know you regret it. But this is your reality.* Our *reality.*

Instead, I asked, "How is he?"

"How am I supposed to know?" she snapped. "They won't tell me anything."

"Have you held him?"

"No. They won't let me touch him. They are acting like I tried to kill him."

I wanted to scream that her actions *could* have killed him, but my words would have complicated things even more.

"Some women keep calling the nurses' station," she told me. "They all want information about how me and the baby are doing so they can give it to the father. They're saying they're my family. Bullshit they are. I didn't even put his father's name on the birth certificate. He's not around and doesn't care. I think he got arrested anyway for unpaid tickets or something. Who knows. What I do know is that *I didn't try to kill my baby.*"

Again, I didn't engage—in a discussion about her addiction or the baby's father. I moved the conversation to her new son's name.

Nanny had already given her opinion, along with all of the reasons for the names she preferred. "That boy will need a name that will get him a job," she'd said. "Something that people can pronounce. Something biblical, like Isaac or Jacob or David. You don't want to confuse anyone with some hard-to-pronounce name." I'd had my thoughts, too. I favored a name he could be proud of, like Kai or Jackson.

My mother wanted something edgier, like Tyrek or Kamari.

Each one of these name discussions ended with my mom saying, "He is my baby. I will name him what I want."

At the hospital, when she'd signed his birth certificate, she misspelled his name as Johnatan. In the end, though, we'd all agreed to spell it the traditional way: Jonathan.

While we talked that day, Jonathan lay in a plastic crib in the maternity ward, the third baby born to my mother with a positive toxicology test. The cocaine levels on Jonathan's report were so high that he would remain with Child Protective Services unless a family member would take him—part of what New York State calls the kinship guardianship assistance program, also known as KinGAP.

THOUGH SHE STILL could not live with or be alone with Jonathan due to her drug use, kinship guardianship would give her the opportunity to see her son. If someone in the family would step up, Jonathan would not have to go to foster care and live with strangers.

Every part of my heart knew Jonathan was meant to be with me.

Maybe it was because I didn't want him passed around like my siblings and I had been. Maybe it was because I didn't want him to get caught up in the foster system, never to be seen again. Maybe it was because of the guilt I felt about not helping my mother a few months before, when she was pregnant and living in her car. Maybe it was because I wanted to give him a fair shot at having a good life, void of drugs, prison, and my mother's neglectful ways.

Still, I worried. Would taking on the responsibility of raising Jonathan as my own feel to my mother that I was punishing her for the mistakes she made with me? Was I?

The idea played over and over in my head as I pushed through the double doors and headed to the nursery to see him for the very first time. I had that feeling that most new mothers have, that he belonged to me and I belonged to him. When I saw him through the plexiglass, I heard only the sound of my heart, each beat a reminder that I was living through this for him. A reminder that we would be okay, and that I could be enough for him. I ignored what I knew would be Nanny's concern: that I was a recent college graduate and shouldn't have to give up my life.

For a preemie, Jonathan was chunky. He had soft skin, my mother's round nose and full lips, and eyes I'd have to wait to see, as he was now sleeping in my arms. I ran my finger over his forehead, down his chubby cheek, and held his small body close to mine. I put my ear next to his little nose, close enough to hear his baby purr. At that moment, it felt like I was holding a piece of my mother, too. I could almost hear her call me Mama as I stood there, legs stiff. I wondered if he'd call me Mama one day, a title I'd welcome only if my mother decided to choose drugs over him.

I knew my mother would be upset with my suggestion that she let me raise Jonathan. Of course I wanted her to get better—I'd wanted that my entire life—but in the twenty-four years I'd been her daughter, she hadn't figured out how to fight off her demons or accept her responsibilities as a mother. She wasn't ready for the job—not at eighteen, when she'd had me, or at forty-one, when she'd had Jonathan.

In the NICU, I held him closer and whispered the words I always wanted to hear my mother say: "Hey, you've got me. I am not going anywhere. We will be together forever. You will never have to worry."

Jonathan slept peacefully, and I watched his chest move up and down. In my mind, I could hear my aunts and uncles, my grandparents, and my mother trying hard to talk me out of stepping up to the task should my mother's situation detour her. Even before seeing Jonathan for the first time, I had known I would need a plan to prove to everyone that I could be his person. I'd need help—and first I'd need to win the trust of Aunt Lady.

"I can move into your house and take care of him for a little while. You don't have to do anything," I had said to her over the phone on my drive to the hospital.

"I for damn sure ain't taking care of another one of Lisa's kids. I am not doing it. I did Danny and Ciara. Hell no," she said in response, exhaustion in her voice as she remembered that her home had been the pit stop between CPS and where my other siblings eventually landed, with Nanny and Poppy.

When I returned to my mother's hospital room, Lady was there. She greeted me with a hug and a suspicious look, the kind of shade that only my aunt can give. Assuming her usual position as rescuer, she had it all under control. I hugged and kissed my mother on the cheek, wanting to feel connected but falling short. The nurses who walked in and out looked at me and my aunt, probably wondering if we were drug users, too.

"How are you feeling?" I asked my mother.

"How do you think I'm feeling?" she shot back. She was angry at herself, and at the situation with the baby's father, but she was taking it out on me.

"Nikki is just trying to help you. She deserves some answers. We all do," Lady said gently.

My mother's demeanor softened slightly, a look of defeat on her face.

I decided not to ask any more questions. Instead, I just tried to be there for her while she managed the emotional and physical pain of having given birth under these circumstances. I let the washcloth speak for me as I cleaned her body. I wiped down her thighs and calves, hoping the warmness of the rag would soothe her. Through my actions, I wanted her to feel that I still loved her despite my own anger. Holding the washcloth tightly, I wondered if my mother remembered when I was born.

JUST LIKE MY newborn baby brother, I came early—three months before my due date, too early for anyone to have prepared for my arrival. I weighed one pound ten ounces, which in 1982 meant there was a high likelihood I would be disabled in some way—developmentally behind or physically impaired, or both.

My parents were just teenagers when they had me, and my family quickly dubbed me their "miracle baby."

My grandmother's sister, Aunt Mary, was a lanky, skinny, light-skinned woman, who had donned a dark-brown wig for as long as I'd known her. The wig served as a kind of armor, I suppose, later used to cover up her thinning, graying hair. She was the one who stayed at my side as I lay in the incubator in the neonatal unit. I'm told her slender fingers, accented by her natural long nails, were the ones that pressed the buttons on the phone to call my grandparents when I stopped breathing at just ten days old.

Despite a few more respiratory setbacks, eventually I thrived. The breathing tubes kept me alive and, later, braces kept my legs straight. Surprising everyone, even the doctors, I crawled, walked, talked, and ate like other kids my age. Still, throughout my early childhood, worries bubbled up inside of Nanny and Poppy with every cough, every fever, every sniffle.

I can only ever wonder if my mother shared those same fears—she was definitely not around to wipe my nose, give me Tylenol, or remind me to cover my mouth when I coughed. For ten years, I lived with my grandparents, as if I were their only child, that is, until my mother gave birth to my brother, Danny, and he eventually moved in with us, too.

Though I was slow to gain weight, I made up for it over the years, indulging in my favorite foods, sure to clean every plate. I learned that food could be there for me in ways that people could not, a lesson I would need to unlearn as an adult.

When my mother was little, she got the nickname Gut, because without fail she would fill her stomach every hour. "She would eat at four p.m. and then again at five p.m.," Uncle Wayne once told me. "Anything she could get her lips around." She enjoyed breakfast the most: toast, bacon, and a bowl of oatmeal swimming in butter and brown sugar. Food didn't let her down in the same way humans did, and if it did, next time she would choose a better option, a better meal. Before she turned to drugs, that was how my mother coped.

In the hospital, I looked at my mother, battered by years of drug use, failed relationships, and nights spent behind bars. I thought about the fighter in me, about how perhaps the reason I was saved at birth was for this very moment—to be Jonathan's anchor. My life was saved so I could be the one to save him, to protect him from the demons that followed both of his parents, the court appearances, the trauma, and the instability of a sad and messy childhood.

I was so very different from my mother, who was social—a partyer, after all—and I usually chose to be alone over hanging out with friends or family. I knew that in order to be Jonathan's anchor, I would need to anchor myself, and that being alone, left to my solitude, would not be good for him. I needed a support system, though asking for any help at all was a foreign concept to me.

There, in the hospital, after that first visit with my mother and my newborn baby brother, I realized it wasn't enough for me to simply *be* different from her. I had to *prove* I was different. Not being an ex-con or not having a drug addiction gave me a solid head start, but would that be enough to convince Child Protective Services, or my own family, that I could do this? I didn't yet have infant clothes to dress Jonathan or formula to feed him, but I did have family members who, if I just asked, would help.

3

IN THE WINTER of 2005, just after my twenty-third birthday and a year before Jonathan was born, I took the train to the place my mother then called home—Bayview Correctional Facility, a medium-security prison across from Chelsea Piers on the west side of New York City. She had been serving time for selling drugs—a crime she said she was framed for—and was being released early on good behavior, after serving three years of her six-year sentence. Her sentence had begun at the county jail in Riverhead before she was moved upstate to Albion prison. Bayview was her last stop.

I can still remember the drug raid that landed her there.

Uncle Wayne called Aunt Lady to share the news that the house on Vail Avenue was being raided. He was too scared to verify the information himself by driving past the house, so I grabbed my car keys and went to confirm the story for myself.

Blue, red, and white lights flashed as I turned onto Vail Avenue. The house was green with a painted white roof. It stood out because it was the only one on the left side of the road, the only one with a sandy driveway. The cool night air caught my tears midstream as I wondered what the cops were saying and doing to my mother. She was four months pregnant with my sister at the time, and my mother and the father came out in handcuffs.

My mother, who had recently ended the relationship, later told me she'd returned that night only to pack her things up. Their relationship had been fierce and volatile, fueled by their equally hot tempers.

That night, I saw many familiar faces as people filed out of the house, their hands and feet shackled to the people behind and in front of them. Frozen in the shadows, I wondered what would happen after they were placed in the big black police vans that lined the street. It was hard to make sense of what I was witnessing, but I wondered if my mother was scared, and if so, how her unborn child would be affected by that fear. I contemplated whether *I* could endure any more visits to the jail, and what we would tell my then-nine-year-old brother, Danny, about his mother this time around.

The brother of my mother's boyfriend stood next to me, whispering quietly. He spoke derisively about his brother, about his brother's addiction, and, inadvertently, about my mother. "They knew what they were doing in that house. It was only a matter of time," he said.

Eventually, every person who stepped into the police vans that night would become an inmate at the Riverhead Correctional Facility. The charges were heavy and complicated, and my mother would need a lawyer. She would need strength.

She decided not to go to trial, took a plea deal, and was given the three-to-six-year sentence.

I knew that my mother's third child—my sister, Ciara—would be born in prison unless we were able to pay bail to get her out of jail while she waited at home for her sentence to start. I had some money from a settlement years earlier, and now I, along with my grandparents and my mother's boyfriend, put up the bail, and the judge believed my mother's promise that she would not flee. Together, we changed the course of my sister's birth story, one that would never involve prison.

A 2023 REPORT by the Prison Policy Initiative, an organization that seeks to end mass criminalization, found that in the United States almost 173,00 women and girls were incarcerated, and that of those, about 80 percent were mothers. As my train chugged along the Hudson River to Bayview that day, my mother was minutes away from being released on parole and joining the more than eight hundred thousand other women who are on parole or probation and under the supervision of the criminal justice system.

As the train approached the city, the anxiety and anticipation of seeing her began to build. I'd visited my mother there before with Nanny, Poppy, and Ciara, and I knew what to expect. Maybe the most gut-wrenching experience of all of my years of going to visit my mother in prison was watching my little sister greet her when she walked into the visiting area. I thought about it now. Ciara did not call her Mom but instead called her Lisa, just as she had heard the guards do.

By the time she turned two years old, my sister knew what to expect on a prison or jail visit. She knew that once she arrived, she had to be on her best behavior. She knew that the men and women standing behind the desk had more authority than her nanny and poppy. She knew that once she made it successfully through the metal detectors, she had to stretch out her arms, then she had to extend both of her arms up and straight out from her body, like the letter *T*. She knew she had to use the bathroom before going in, because she was only allowed one diaper per visit.

If Poppy had come along, with money in his wallet, she knew she would get candy, chips, or some kind of junk food from the vending machine. She knew how to wait patiently for her mother to come down from her room. She knew that she was allowed to play with the other children but not allowed to run. She knew she would leave her visit with a stamp on her hand. She knew that her mommy would not be going home with her that day.

She knew what it was like to live without her mother. She knew all of this before she was able to read a book. I did, too. But on that cold train trip from upstate New York to New York City, I still had fantasies that my mother could change, had changed. I was forever hopeful.

MY MOTHER'S RELEASE was scheduled for 11 a.m., and I was early. I knocked on the heavy steel door until I saw the dark-brown eyes of an officer staring back at me. A tall, Black man with a deep voice, he let me in and asked me for the name of the person I was there to pick up.

"I'm here for Lisa Eleazer."

The guard looked at me, then down at a pile of papers, then back again, as if I seemed too young to be standing in front of him alone. He handed me a form acknowledging my mother's release to me, and one glide of the pen gave her freedom and me a human being to care for. My heart began to race. Had I made a mistake coming here instead of Nanny? What was I doing? Wasn't this the job of her mother?

Mostly, release day was about waiting. Waiting for my mother to get medical clearance. Waiting for her to gather up her belongings. I already felt like I had been waiting for her all my life. I leaned against the cement wall and peeked through the square hole in the door. I thought about the classes I had missed and the lies I had told about my weekend plans when I was really coming to see her. My college years were often interrupted by the voice of a telephone operator when I would receive a call from her from jail.

This is Bayview Correctional Facility. You have a call from . . .

To accept, press . . .

I never got used to those calls.

It felt like an eternity passed before my mother was hopping down the stairs toward me. She had on a sweatsuit the color of mustard and was smiling. Relief consumed me, to know we'd both be leaving this prison. But my limp arms and grim expression gave away another feeling, one I couldn't hide—that I was less than thrilled to be there. I wasn't at all ready to welcome her back home or into my life. I had no idea if we could ever make up for lost time. Or if we would be repeating this process in six months or a year.

My mother fell into me with the warmest hug I'd ever received from her. I focused on what I did know: we had today, and that's all I could guarantee—this moment, her hug, and our mutual relief that she was getting out of this place.

"Okay, Lisa, we better not see you here again," the officer said, his eyebrows arching upward as he spoke. "I need you to sign these papers. You have a check coming to you for the work you did while you were here."

"You might as well keep it," my mother said. "And you don't have to worry—you won't be seeing me again. I am going to get my life back, and my kids back, too."

TWO MONTHS AFTER my mother's release, I graduated from Bard, leaving behind the stability and comfort I'd known as a student. My dark-skinned, five-foot-tall self with braided hair boldly walked across the stage to accept my bachelor's degree and shake the hand of the bow-tie-clad president of the college. I was scared to be going into the unknown, but I thought my future looked promising.

My mother, still fresh out of prison, was in the audience to watch me that day. She was sweating profusely in the pink outfit my grandmother had bought her especially for the occasion. She herself had dropped out of high school in the tenth grade and had never understood how much I valued my education. I'm not sure if she knew how much the support of my family meant to me. She'd already missed my high school graduation, and I practically took her by the hand and led her to this one, just so I could say she was there.

Four years earlier, when I'd arrived at Bard for the very first time—stepping onto the nearly one thousand acres that make up the college campus, in the middle of nowhere, with the closest grocery store a ten-minute car ride away—it felt like I'd finally found my home. There, among the trees and the hidden waterfalls and the quirky kids who climbed those trees between classes and who had a lot to say in freshman seminar, was where I belonged. I built a community of friends, gravitating toward the school's queer students.

My first-year roommate was quiet but supportive; she was interested in my life and asked me questions about my relationships. But only my closest friends knew where my mother was and what she had done. I shared with them the secret but was too ashamed to tell most others who came in and out of my life. And it wasn't until my final year that I wrote about it: for my senior thesis I researched families dealing with an incarcerated loved one—families like mine.

At Bard, there were people who had money and came from backgrounds very different from my own. I went to school with the sons and daughters of celebrities. I knew I was different, but not solely because my family couldn't afford the tuition or because my skin color was darker than 90 percent of the student body. I was different because my mother was a criminal.

I was admitted to Bard as part of New York State's Higher Education Opportunity Program, which gives students with potential the chance to enroll in college, especially if they've had less-than-stellar academic histories—like if they had lower grades because, say, they had to be a caregiver for a family member instead of going to class consistently—or they can't afford college tuition and other expenses. I'd soon find out that some people looked down on HEOP students, assuming we got some kind of extra-special treatment. I kept my focus on what I could control and did not bother with what I couldn't. I felt lucky that I had the chance to build relationships with people I am still friends with to this very day. I didn't feel like the "other" because I was a student in the program, though I know some of my peers did. Whatever otherness I may have perceived being thrown my way from a few of my more privileged white peers paled in comparison to the otherness of having a mother in prison.

Early on, the only person who knew about my mother was my friend Betsaida. As we walked together to the campus cafeteria for dinner one night, she shared a story about her own family. As she allowed herself to be vulnerable with me, I drifted into my own head, my heart slowing down, easing with each breath. My thoughts sped through my mind as if I were on some roller-coaster ride, clinging to the bar, as I contemplated whether or not I should tell her who and where my mother was. As we pulled open the glass door to the commons, I made a decision.

"I am not even sure how to say this."

"Say what?" Betsaida asked.

We stood just inside the entrance as other students bustled around us. I felt my chest tighten up, like my lungs were getting smaller and smaller, making it hard for me to breathe. I tried to inhale before speaking again.

"I never talk about my mom, because she's in jail."

I didn't wait for Betsaida's response. I didn't want to see or hear her feel sorry for me. I walked past her, into the cafeteria.

She followed. "Nikkya, why didn't you tell me sooner? I don't know what I could have done, but at least, I hope, you know you can talk to me."

Betsaida didn't judge me. She became my close friend, and we remained friends all throughout college and long after we graduated. Like me, she was a fighter, proving to all the naysayers that Bard was where she was meant to be; she worked hard and relied on scholarships, too. Even if her mother wasn't in jail like mine, as an immigrant from the Dominican Republic, Betsaida understood me and what it was like to face challenges. Betsaida and I graduated together, and on commencement day, her mother and her father were there to witness her success, grateful for the opportunity she had been given to attend a place like Bard.

I had my papers, the ones that would admit me to a future that I deserved. I felt proud of my determination to go to college, to graduate, to take concrete steps toward the life I had dreamed about, to make connections with people who accepted me *and* where I had come from. I had accomplished this on my own, and no one—no cop, no judge, no nonexistent parent—could take that away from me.

I don't know what my mother was thinking as she watched me that day. My mother had a Class D felony instead of a high school diploma or a college degree. It was a criminal record that she would carry through the rest of her life. In some ways, my degree equipped me to right my mother's wrongs, to defy her legacy.

AFTER GIVING BIRTH to Jonathan, after telling off the CPS workers, after yelling at doctors and nurses that she hadn't tried to harm her baby, after signing his birth certificate and misspelling his name, my mother was done parenting her newborn son. She stood in a blue-and-white checkered hospital gown that barely covered her round body, watching as I murmured in Jonathan's ear and showered him with kisses, dressing him to leave the hospital without her.

My mother was in a precarious situation with her health. Her heart trouble, her asthma, her obesity, her C-section, along with her drug addiction, made it necessary for her to stay in the hospital longer. A makeshift plan had been worked out. My family was against my sacrificing my midtwenties to commit to raising Jonathan and opposed to my helping my mother this much. But it was no longer about her; it was about Jonathan's well-being. I went against Nanny and Poppy's wishes and moved in with Aunt Lady so that I could take care of Jonathan. Technically, she had agreed to be Jonathan's temporary guardian, speaking with CPS and signing any paperwork needed, but on the verbal condition that I would do the heavy lifting: waking up with him, feeding him, changing his diapers.

Aunt Lady and I had bought newborn clothes from The Children's Place at the outlet mall two miles away, the same place

I'd worked in high school. We filled our navy-blue fabric shopping bag with a light-blue jacket, some onesies, socks, and a few cotton sleepers. With each piece of clothing I put into the bag, I felt a sense of joy, of giddiness.

I WAS GIVING this baby a chance. I was stepping in as his mother. I could not let myself be scared or allow myself the space to think about what I didn't yet know about mothering. I didn't take the time to consider all of the things I didn't have, like my own apartment, money in my bank account, a stable partner by my side, or even a bed of my own. I didn't yet know how hard it was to take care of another human being, especially without many resources.

I'd already gotten Jonathan a new car seat from a thrift store near my grandparents' home. They had a Tuesday special: anything you could fit into a shopping bag for only five dollars. The first week of December, with the car seat locked into position, Aunt Lady and I went to go pick him up.

"Helloooooooo, Jonathan," we cooed in unison. "Today, you're going home."

I held him, cradled his little body in my arms, my face snug against his soft brown head. His dark-brown eyes were open, and he looked at me calmly, no fear to be found. The pediatrician gave him one last check before clearing him for discharge.

"I have no concerns at this time," he said. "Just keep a close eye on him. Babies born as he was, can take a turn."

I was too afraid to look into my mother's eyes while putting Jonathan in his new jacket. I didn't want to see her hurt, to bear witness to her feelings. *Of course she's hurt,* I thought. *Maybe even angry with you. You're doing what she could not.* I was feeling it all as I gave her one last quick goodbye, took Jonathan's little hand, and waved it at her.

As my mother waved back, her thin hospital gown swayed. She was in a familiar place: On the outside looking in, inches away from a life she could never quite access. Emotionally distant, muted by her addictions, incapable of breaking down the barriers between us, wanting to be there but always falling short.

Before we left, I looked back one final time. She stood on the other side of the glass, tears streaming down her face. She was in pain, but I had Jonathan to comfort now.

4

————

ON OUR FIRST night home from the hospital, I had no idea what to expect. Lady helped me, of course, showing me how to open the tiny flaps of a newborn baby's diaper and how to avoid confusing the front with the back. She pointed out where the blue line would appear in the diaper, indicating Jonathan had peed, told me the sure sign of a bowel movement would be the smell. I needed all five of my senses on duty.

As we sat side by side in her dimly lit kitchen, she taught me how to prepare Jonathan's bottle. With each movement, I heard the white linoleum floor creak beneath our feet. Her instructions were given quickly, in keeping with the bluntness of her personality, and her words came through with the confidence of a mother who'd done all of this many, many times.

If he wakes up at night, make sure you don't put him in the bed with you.

Make sure you don't put his diaper on too tight.

You cannot sleep deeply, because you won't hear him cry.

Those first few nights, Jonathan didn't need much more than someone he could count on to feed him, bathe him, clothe him, and keep him safe. My confidence grew with each passing day, while my role in his life went from caregiver to something more. I knew how to attend to his basic needs, but inside, I was conflicted about allowing myself to fully feel like his mother—because his biological mother was very much alive.

Even before he'd been released from the hospital, everything in his short life was already complicated. Child Protective Services, my family, everyone had an opinion about who this tiny baby boy should live with, including me. I wanted him. But nothing about his future could be settled permanently until a decision by CPS about whether my mother could be sober and prove herself capable. So really, at least for now, he legally belonged to the state, even if it was temporary, I hoped.

My grandmother had been especially clear that she did not want me to have the burden of raising my mother's child. Nanny knew the sacrifices I'd need to make—she'd made the same for me. She'd stayed up late with me, comforting me, when I couldn't breathe. She'd provided for me even when she didn't have the money; she'd used credit cards so I would not go without. My grandparents treated me as if they'd birthed me into this world, sacrificing for me and my needs and forgoing their own. Nanny had turned her home into *our* home. She'd done the same for my siblings Danny and Ciara through elementary school, before they both went to live with She-She and her husband, Steve.

As soon as Jonathan was born, my grandmother had begun calling family members across the United States, begging them to take him in and keep him out of foster care. "I cannot raise another one of her kids," I overheard her saying on the phone. "I am getting too old to run after a baby."

I didn't interfere with the calls and requests, but I'd already made plans to fight for Jonathan. I didn't think my mother could mother anyone, but I was still hopeful that I was wrong and thought that maybe, together, we would raise Jonathan.

Lady had already temporarily rescued Danny and Ciara. Danny lived with Lady when CPS took him away from our mother at his birth, but when he was still only months old, my mother took him back. Danny's birth had come at the height of my mother's drug addiction and drug dealing. Placing him in her care was a risk, but she wanted him.

The story, as Aunt Lady shared with me a few times, was that one day she went to visit my mother on the Indian reservation where she lived with Danny and Danny's father. When Lady entered the house, she saw my mother asleep on the couch and Danny, now crawling at about six months old, moving quickly toward the open basement door, seconds away from tumbling headfirst down a flight of stairs. Lady shook my mother hard, waking her from a deep sleep, and yelled at her about how careless and irresponsible she was. Lady took Danny from her that very day.

After about three months of once again living with Lady, Danny moved in with Nanny, Poppy, and me, in Pennsylvania, the place we then called home. Thankfully, he'd not spent any time in a foster home or with a foster parent.

Unlike my own relatively stable childhood with my

grandparents, my brother's and sister's lives resembled a game of tag, no one wanting to truly take responsibility for them, like their very existence was an inconvenience. I didn't want Jonathan to be anybody's inconvenience. I wanted him to know he could always be with me. Parenthood, to me, was about being that constant in the life of a kid. And I was willing to fully commit to Jonathan.

Because Lady had experience in this land of raising a newborn—foreign to me—and because she spoke the language and could communicate in ways that I could not, she agreed to deal with the unrelenting back-and-forth with CPS, which had the ultimate decision-making authority. Reunification, in the agency's eyes, was the end goal, even though the employees there were well aware of my mother's history.

Lady gave me a bedroom in her newly renovated basement apartment, the same room my mother occupied before she relapsed. With its shiny floors, thin walls, fluorescent lights, and ceiling tiles that easily popped out with the slightest push, the space always felt cold and uncomfortable to me. In the living room area, there was an oversized black leather couch flush with the wall, leaving little room to walk to the adjacent bedrooms.

But I was grateful for our temporary home. It would do until I could figure out what was next.

THE SAME WEEK Jonathan came home with us, I received a phone call from the hospital social worker, Ms. Diballo. Her frosty, authoritative tone immediately signaled this would not be a pleasant conversation. She'd been arguing with my mother, who wanted to leave before she'd been medically cleared to do so. The social worker thought a chat with me would change her mind.

"I have your mother here," she said with a long sigh. "She is insisting that she be discharged, but we are not recommending that just yet."

"Can I talk to her?" I asked.

Now I was the authoritative, cold one.

"Why are you trying to leave?" I asked my mother when Ms. Diballo passed the phone to her.

"I am getting out of this hospital. The nurses are being so mean to me. They are treating me worse than a criminal. I am afraid I'll do something to one of them that I will regret."

"Where will you go?"

"I don't know, but I am leaving here. I have enough friends I can stay with, or I can get a hotel room. But not here, Nikkya."

She used my real name—not Mama—when she wanted to remind me that I was hers.

"Okay, if that's your choice, go ahead."

She returned the phone to the social worker.

"Ms. Diballo, I tried talking to her, but she's not in a place to listen to me. She is going to sign herself out," I said matter-of-factly, like a parent whose hands were tied. I felt irritated, stuck once again in the position of attempting to convince my mother to make a wise decision. I was tired of it. "There's nothing I can do. This is her choice, wrong or right."

Frustrated as I was, I wanted to protect my mother from herself so badly. I knew she would call me again once she figured out

where she would go. She would never completely disappear—
unless she was on a drug binge.

Later that night, my mother called me to say she was staying at a motel not far from Aunt Lady's. She told me she'd been
bleeding, a lingering effect of the C-section. She asked if I'd
bring her sanitary napkins and a few towels from Lady's house,
and I quickly agreed. I needed to see with my own two eyes that
she was okay. After Jonathan went to sleep, I lied to my aunt
and told her that I needed to run to the store. The truth would
have brought on a lecture, which I just didn't have the emotional
energy for.

I arrived at the low-budget motel, with its peeling white siding, and called my mother's room. The familiarity of her raspy
voice made me feel sick—was she just exhausted or had she used
drugs again? I could never understand the addiction to cocaine
or money or men, and my mother never offered excuses or reasons for her behaviors. My mother also never said she was sorry,
but she did sometimes admit to her faults. She was who she was,
she said—always just shy of taking responsibility. It would likely
be the same this time.

I walked toward my mother's door and knocked. I handed her
the overstuffed bag I'd packed with the requested items, hugged
her, and held back my tears. She asked for money, and I gave her
the few dollars I had with me. I wanted to stay the night, to be
there to support her, and do what I thought a daughter should
do, but I couldn't. I needed to get back to Jonathan.

Over the next few days, my mother took the first steps to get
her life in order. She contacted her parole officer and told him

she wanted to get into a halfway house to get clean. She connected with friends but stayed away from Jonathan's father, who was in jail because of a DUI. Her voice still hoarse, her body still weak, she called every day to check in on me and Jonathan.

At the start of the new year, when Jonathan was just five weeks old, my mother and I went to an appointment at the Department of Social Services in Riverhead to apply for the Special Supplemental Nutrition Program for Women, Infants, and Children (WIC), a federal program with local offices within each state. This meeting would allow Jonathan to receive formula, and later milk, eggs, and cheese for free. I remember sitting in the car beforehand, feeling ashamed that I couldn't even afford a can of Enfamil. And I couldn't stop thinking about how far removed I was from what I should have been doing with my life as a recent college grad. As much as I loved Jonathan, I still couldn't help but imagine what my life would be like without the responsibility of caring for him. Especially at times like this.

My mother led the way into the building, and I looked around as we entered, my eyes darting from person to person, hoping no one recognized me. During our quick consultation with the intake coordinator, the conversation centered around Jonathan, his needs, and his home life. My mother had done this before— she knew what to expect and had anticipated each question in a way that amazed me.

We left the meeting with vouchers in hand, and at the grocery store she took me straight to the formula aisle. I was overwhelmed by how many varieties there were on the shelves: Enfamil and Similac, Earth's Best, and the store brand. I had no way of decoding which was best, but WIC didn't give us a choice. There were signs underneath each item on the shelf, denoting which brand WIC would pay for. The ones not covered would have the price of the item, but those covered had the letters W-I-C.

We walked through the checkout line together: me, Jonathan, and my mom. My mother was either unaware or didn't care about the white ladies who stood behind us, but I felt their stares, the same kind I'd get in church when I was doing something others thought I shouldn't be. I knew that I was now doing what was necessary, but like I had as a child, I avoided their disapproving eyes as I passed the voucher to the cashier.

This cannot be my life, I thought. *This is not the life I want for Jonathan.*

"Pick your lip up," my mother said when she saw my mouth hanging open.

Back at the car, I buckled Jonathan into his car seat and kissed him on his forehead while his curly baby Afro tickled my face. I doubted that I would ever get used to asking for this kind of help, relying on paper checks to provide such a basic need. I knew this would never feel right or normal to me. But I got behind the wheel, my mother in the passenger seat, and we started to drive.

Each month from then on, I dutifully showed up at my WIC appointment for my vouchers, and each time the grocery store conveyor belt pushed the cans closer to the till, my hands began to sweat in anticipation that the cashier would judge me. Each time, I'd find a different cashier, worried that otherwise they'd remember me, come to see me as "that woman." Would the cashier ask me questions that I could not answer? Would she write me off as another young Black mother who couldn't afford to buy food for her baby? Did she wonder where the dad was—in jail, dead, or a deadbeat?

While the US Department of Agriculture reported that more than six million women, infants, and children of all races were enrolled in WIC in 2023, Black women have long been pegged as the ones who always need help—the ones who are waiting for a government handout, unwilling to work, baby-making machines trying to support their fatherless children on welfare. But other than my mother, that was not the story of any of the Black women in my family. We didn't stand in line for this kind of help. And yet I found myself standing here with my WIC vouchers while old white ladies behind me spewed audible sighs because I was holding up the line.

They didn't know my story, and maybe they never would.

5

———

ABOUT A MONTH after Jonathan's birth, I experienced another first—my first time in family court.

I was there to support my mother, who needed to show the judge she'd made enough progress to regain custody of her child. She was both confident and concerned—her past appearances in front of a judge, while for different reasons, had scarred her. Everything about her that day told me she wasn't ready. She wasn't dressed for court. She didn't carry a handbag. She didn't own business attire or heels. Instead, she chose to wear a matching red sweatsuit, her favorite color, accompanied by a red bubble jacket.

The ways in which my mother fed her addiction left others, most often her family, desperate for her to change, to get better, to stop using and selling drugs. She'd forged stolen checks and taken Aunt Lady's social security number, using her identity when she was pulled over by the cops. She'd lived in so many different places with so many different random people—people she would call "friends," people I would meet and then never see again.

My mother once told me that the other women she'd been to rehab with were not like her.

"Those girls sold their bodies," she said. "They slept with men to get their next fix. I could never sell my body for a piece of crack." By then, I'd hit a point in my relationship with my mother in which I questioned every statement she made, but I was still too afraid to know the truth.

Jonathan had slept in his car seat next to me in the waiting area while inside, my mother told me when she walked out of the courtroom, she had vowed to the judge that this time, for this child, it would be different. She said she swore to the judge that she did not know the crack she smoked the night she went into labor was laced with another drug. Then she plopped down in the chair, pulled her red bubble jacket around her, and cried.

I waited for a beat and then held her to me, wondering why she hadn't fought like this for me all these years ago. Or maybe she had. Either way, I wanted her to borrow some tools from my toolbox now, ones that would help her become the mother she wanted to be to Jonathan. I wanted her to have my determination to keep him out of the foster care system, something she'd clearly failed to think about when she chose to get high. I wanted to believe she wanted Jonathan back. I wanted to believe she would finally be clean for somebody, even if she could never be clean for me.

But I also knew when Jonathan looked at me, when he wrapped his chubby hand around my finger or laid his round head in the crook of my neck, that we had an unbreakable bond. Though I didn't share with anyone what I felt, I knew that we had somehow chosen each other, had heard each other's spirit call. We were the family we needed.

IN JANUARY 2007, when Jonathan was two months old, my mother entered a drug rehabilitation center, a necessary step before she could apply for placement in a halfway house. She would need to commit to a program in order to be deemed fit to care for Jonathan. This was a test for herself, for CPS, for all of us.

Aunt Lady's daughter, Natasha, was on winter break from her college, so she volunteered to come with me as I drove for an hour and a half in the snow to visit my mother at South Oaks Hospital in Amityville, New York. Natasha and I are the same age and have been inseparable our entire lives. We both came home the same day from the hospital and into my grandparents' home, a safe place for two newborns while our then young mothers went out and partied together.

Natasha and I were different in so many ways. She was tall. I was short. She was skinny. I was chubby. She was light-skinned. I was dark-skinned. She had long, straight hair pulled back in a tight ponytail, while mine was permed and styled with hard plastic curlers. She would speak her mind and roll her big brown eyes when someone irritated her. I, on the other hand, was always in my head, thinking through every word, too afraid to stand up for myself. She was considered the "pretty Black girl," and whenever I looked into a mirror, I saw my skin, my oily hair, my crooked smile. And the most important difference between us: Natasha's mother eventually accepted responsibility for her daughter. My mother abandoned me.

Natasha had always had a bond with my mother, though, and she showed her love more than I did. To Natasha, my mother was just Lisa—the cool aunt who she could share secrets with, who would tell it like it was and wouldn't take any bullshit. Even in old pictures, Natasha and my mother hold each other close—so close that I am unsure of where my mother's face ends and Natasha's begins. In the few baby photos of me that exist, I always look like I am trying to escape my mother's grasp, as if I am untrusting of the stranger who holds me in her arms.

Now, with baby Jonathan in tow, Natasha and I entered the psychiatric ward where the drug rehab program was situated. I knew the routine when visiting jails and prisons, and at rehab it was only slightly different. There were no metal detectors at the center, no bars to separate us but there was a lock on the outside door, keeping family and friends out and the addicts in. My mother had gone to rehab before and had been unsuccessful. I'd heard the stories from her brothers and sisters, all too weary of her failures to visit her this time around.

I had brought with me a bag of things my mother had requested: some clothes, mail that had been sent to Lady's house from family court, five dollars in quarters so she could have access to the pay phone, and five dollars in cash so she could buy cigarettes. My fingers gripped the handles of the large bag as my cousin and I walked to the reception desk.

"What are you going to do with that baby?" the receptionist asked us. "There are no babies allowed at visitation."

Natasha took Jonathan back to the car. I watched her as she struggled to navigate the car seat while holding the door open wide enough for them both. Once I saw that they were inside the car, I turned back toward the receptionist. We exchanged no words; with the baby gone, she buzzed me in.

The heavy door locked behind me, and when I entered the large room I was blinded by the bright-red carpeted floors. I felt completely disoriented. There was an eerie quietness. The only person in this massive room was walking directly toward me. That person was my mother.

A smile lit up my mom's face as she stretched out her arms to hug me. Tight against her body, I could smell her deodorant, and I pulled back as she leaned in for a kiss, worried her red lipstick would stain my face. Her skin seemed brighter, and she had a pep in her walk.

Unsure of what I was feeling—perhaps a mix of excitement and frustration—I followed her to a sitting room filled with chairs with wooden armrests and gray cushions. The red carpet hurt my eyes if I stared at it too long. The handful of other women there spoke in hushed tones.

"How you doin', Mama?" she asked, not waiting for me to respond. "I'm so glad you were able to make it, even if for a short time. It's good to see you."

All I could muster was meek agreement. I wanted to be happy to see her, but I wore my anger like a coat of armor, false protection from any future pain she might cause me. She hugged me again as if I'd forgiven her, but I hadn't. I think I was still waiting for an apology from her, a sorry for not being there for me or for

Jonathan. But the words never came. Underneath the anger, too, I still felt scared that she would relapse or she would get pregnant again or she would die the next time she chose to do drugs.

I was relieved when our ten minutes were up.

"MAN, I HOPE we don't need to come back to this place," I told Natasha as soon as I got back into the car.

"She'll be fine. This is just a hump she has to get over. She will."

My cousin's words were meant to be comforting—encouraging, even. But she would never understand the shame I felt visiting my mother in one facility after another.

"She wants to do right this time," Natasha continued. "She does. So let's believe she will."

Two weeks after my mom entered rehab, a bed opened up at a halfway house, and she moved in as soon as she was discharged from the rehab facility, about a month later. It was a tan split-level ranch on the same street where Karl, Jonathan's father, lived. I wondered if this was a premeditated plan on my mother's part to rebuild the family that had been broken.

I had never met Karl, only knew him through the stories my mother told about their brief relationship. She said that he had cheated on his common-law wife with my mom and that at first he denied Jonathan was his son, claiming that he had not in fact committed adultery and accusing my mother of sleeping around—anything to avoid taking responsibility.

The halfway house had a small front yard of brown grass struggling to grow, a metaphor for those living inside. My mother's housemates, seven white women, were all recovering from alcohol or drug abuse. On weekends, Jonathan and I would visit. At first, it was out of obligation, but soon I began to look forward to it. It was the most one-on-one time I'd ever had with my mother in my entire life.

During our visits, I watched her closely. I noticed that her nostrils flared every time she talked, and wondered if mine did the same. I had spent so much time trying to deny I shared any traits with my mother, but now I realized there were similarities between us, like how much she loved potato chips, and how strong and sturdy her forearm was when I touched it, and how tidy she kept her room. Her lotions, perfumes, and hair combs were all neatly displayed on her nightstand, everything close and within eyesight, as if she didn't have an entire room to hold her things; she'd been conditioned to live like she was still behind bars.

Seeing joy and laughter on her face, and no longer defeat, gave me a glimpse of what my own childhood could have been. I was living out this dream through Jonathan's eyes. And for once, I didn't feel angry.

When Jonathan and I would arrive, she'd scoop him from his car seat, hold him tight, and lead us through the house, past the dated kitchen with its linoleum floor and cheap yellow countertops. She'd take us down a narrow carpeted staircase with a metal handrail and into another carpeted room with a television. The damp basement smell lingered in the underground room that tried to double as a cozy den, a failed attempt at providing comfort. My mother would sit on the brown couch that was covered in a fabric that made my skin itch. I would sit diagonally across from her and Jonathan, watching her every move as if she were on a supervised visit. In some ways, she was.

In the beginning I was critical of her, and sometimes I voiced my thoughts. When she would hold him on one knee, my stomach would clench in fear that his little body wasn't strong enough to hold his own weight. When she'd bounce him up and down, coo at him, bend down and rub her nose against his, sing to him during the commercials of whatever Lifetime movie we were watching, I would complain. "You're going to spoil him. Then I have to deal with the crying," I'd say.

She would give me an eyeroll and maybe a sigh, but she would never argue or disagree with me. Maybe she was too tired to fight with anyone anymore. The most she'd do is shoot a dig at me—"Lookin' just like your father, look at you"—if I said something that got to her. I wondered if my looking like my father was somehow part of the reason my mother hadn't shown up for me. Through my aunts and uncles, I'd learned how he'd hurt her, beating her with his fists and knocking her down with his words, but she told me she loved him anyway.

The night my mother decided to leave my father was the night she decided he had hit her for the last time. When I was two years old, my parents had wanted to try out being a family of three. My father enlisted in the army and was sent to basic training in Texas. My mother and I moved out of my grandparents' house and in with him. My mother became an army wife, and I became a military brat.

One night, my mother was frying a chicken dinner at the

stove, preparing for my father to return from his shift on the base. Whenever my mother would recall the story, her voice would trail off, and I'd be left to fill in the blanks. I'd pieced together enough to figure out that while my mother was cooking, somehow a piece of hot grease hit my bare skin, landing in the space between my shoulder blades and the arch of my back. I cried out in pain as my skin sizzled like a piece of raw meat. My mother picked me up and tried to calm me down, wiping tears from my cheeks. When my father, very likely drunk, opened the front door and saw the scene, he was furious. "What happened to her, Lisa?" he screamed. I can only imagine the fear my mother must have felt as she put me down and braced herself for what would come next. He smacked her, and it escalated.

Neither my mother nor I ever returned to Texas or my father's home again.

EVENTUALLY I LEARNED to hold my tongue instead of sharing my opinions on how my mother was interacting with Jonathan during our visits at the halfway house. Each weekend, I got to know her a little more and I began to soften.

"He's my baby," she would say. "I want to hold him. You get him all the time."

And she was right.

For two months, weekend after weekend, the three of us sat together on that same brown tattered sofa. Sometimes she played with Jonathan. Sometimes she and I talked. Sometimes we'd just watch TV. She'd look at me, and I'd look back, no words spoken but sharing in the knowledge that we were there for each other.

We were in the moment. She was available to Jonathan and, by extension, to me. As I watched my mother transforming from the old Lisa into a woman I began to respect, I was able to smile.

A few weeks after my mother entered the halfway house, we had gone to family court. The judge did not terminate my mother's parental rights, but rather transferred custody to me, and out of Lady's hands. After the transfer of custody was official, my mother and I sat in silence in the waiting area while the clerk prepared the order.

As CPS saw it, my mother needed a bit longer to prove herself a viable, healthy, stable option for Jonathan. She was heading in the right direction, and I reassured my mom that my custody of Jonathan would only last until she was ready, though I still questioned it myself.

"Nikkya, I am gonna get my baby back," she said. "You can have him now—I have no problem with that—but just don't get too attached."

Her words stung. I was already attached, had been attached before he was born. Plus, I wanted nothing more than to offer Jonathan someone to be attached to. My daydreams were about how I'd be involved in his life: if we'd live down the road from my mother as she continued to rehabilitate herself or if she'd vanish from both of our lives altogether, leaving me to be more than his half sister. His well-being, his emotional and physical health—these were my first concerns in the morning and my last at night.

Although her words hurt, I was not mad and I was not sad. Even if her intention was to put me in my place, to make sure I knew who Jonathan's mother really was, I understood. She loved Jonathan. And so did I. She was trying to do better as a mother. She changed his diapers whenever we were together. She fed him. She sang to him. She showed him she cared.

She became a regular at Narcotics Anonymous meetings and resigned herself to me being Jonathan's temporary guardian.

6

WITH MY TEMPORARY custody papers in hand and Jonathan turning two months old, I decided to move into my great-uncle Bubby's house, just a couple miles away from Aunt Lady's.

Bubby was my grandmother's older brother and the kindest and gentlest of souls. He wore long johns year-round, loved his job in animal control, and had the baldest, shiniest head I'd ever seen. He was also a man who believed that life could be hard, but with God, there was nothing we could not make it through. Nanny once told me that he had been a very wild teenager, but I couldn't quite imagine it. He used the word *good* in just about every sentence. Bad things seemed not to exist in his world, even though I knew bad things had happened to him.

Uncle Bubby stoically fought his own demons, including the trauma of losing his younger brother in a car accident. The pair were in a pickup truck winding down the tiny country roads in Cartersville, Virginia, Uncle Bubby behind the wheel. He was speeding—perhaps being that wild teenager—and having fun with his brother, who was hanging out the passenger-side window. At some point, their pickup and a lumber truck nicked each other, and Robert was crushed between the two vehicles.

It was a horrific way to die, and I never heard Nanny, Uncle Bubby, or any of their siblings talk about the event in one another's presence. They mostly stuffed their feelings inside. For my family, and so many others like my own, it was God who they turned their troubles over to. And for Uncle Bubby, God became a guiding light.

Uncle Bubby's house on Lincoln Street was old, but we had more space than we did in Lady's basement. Bright yellow with a squeaky metal fence, it sat on a corner in historic Riverhead, in a part of town where Polish immigrants had settled long before Uncle Bubby had. The yard, without flowers or green grass, was instead filled with broken tools that Bubby hoped to get around to fixing, and cages to catch and trap squirrels and raccoons—part of his one-man "wildlife removal service." With four bedrooms and two bathrooms, we were able to sidestep the stacks of old newspapers and antiques that were piled up everywhere.

Uncle Bubby's street had been a refuge for Nanny. It was where she had first moved with her children after that rainy night back in the '70s when her then husband became physical. She eventually found a second-story apartment on Lincoln Street, where the family shared bedrooms and a single bathroom—a cramped space for Lady, Wayne, Kendra, She-She, Main, and my mother—but they were happy they were together. Uncle Bubby's house was just up the road, and his kids and Nanny's would play together for hours in Bubby's backyard until they were called inside for dinner. Now, thirty years after my aunts and uncles had left Lincoln Street, I was back.

Uncle Bubby would start each day with a bright smile and a silly joke, then wipe his nose with a dingy handkerchief he kept in his shirt pocket. When I entered the room with Jonathan, he'd reach out to catch Jonathan's tiny nose between his thumb and his index finger. Bubby's small kitchen was overtaken by dirty dishes, expired boxes of Special K, and linens that had a film of dust on them from never being touched. For breakfast, he offered us what he had every morning: a fried egg, bacon, and toast.

Our rooms were up a set of winding stairs, the kind you'd see in an old Victorian house in the movies. Jonathan and I occupied a rarely used bedroom and bathroom at the end of a narrow hallway. The two small windows provided the bedroom with very little sunlight, and a speckled red quilt covered the bed. I pushed the bed flush against the wood-paneled wall, giving Jonathan protection from falling out if he slept next to me. Most nights, I put him to sleep in his playpen, a green-and-tan Pack 'n Play gifted to us by my aunt Eva, and while it wasn't the sturdy cherry-oak crib I'd wanted him to have, it served our needs until I could afford something better.

Once we were settled, the heaviness of our new situation hit me; we now called my great-uncle's cluttered house home because we had nowhere else to go. Lady's house had been a layover, and although I was grateful to both of them, I prayed that Uncle Bubby's would be temporary, too.

I dreamed of a future home for us, with flowers lining the walkway and a beautiful yard Jonathan could run around in.

FOR AS LONG as I've been able to drive, I have been my mother's chauffeur. I only have one memory of her ever being in the driver's seat while I was in the car. I was about eight or nine at the time, my skinny legs sticking to the black leather back seat, no seat belt around my waist. I vividly remember the quiet in the car after she'd said to me "Lookin' just like your father," a line she would repeat so often over the years that I'd grow to resent it. It hadn't become a sore point yet, and I was feeling happy. My mother sang along to Gloria Gaynor's "I Will Survive." I guess we were surviving my mother's addiction together.

The second week in February 2007, one night after a weekend visit with my mother, she called from her halfway house and asked me to take her to the hospital. I made the twenty-minute drive from Bubby's house, and when I got there, she walked slowly toward my car. Her skin looked gray.

"My chest hurts," she said.

I remained with her at the hospital until the doctor returned with inconclusive results and told us my mother would need to stay the night for further observation. He looked at me nervously, then at my mother. It was clear he was unsure if he should ask his question in front of me, but he eventually did anyway.

"I know you gave birth recently and tested positive for cocaine. Did cocaine bring you into the emergency room tonight?"

She rolled her eyes and smacked her lips.

"I did not use drugs. And anything you have to say to me, you can say in front of my daughter. I have nothing to hide from her or from you."

After a couple of long hours in the ER, I returned home to

Uncle Bubby's. My eyes watered from exhaustion, and my body ached to lie down. I checked on Jonathan, giving him a quick kiss on his cheek while he slept.

Had my mother lied to me and the doctor? Did she relapse?

I picked up Jonathan from his playpen and put him in the bed beside me. The house was peaceful, and I could hear the hum of his breaths. I held his little hand in mine. When I leaned over to turn off the light, my phone rang.

"I'm leaving," my mother said without even a hello.

"What happened? Why?"

"Can you pick me up?"

"Did they say you could leave?"

"Can you just come and take me home?"

I was worn-out, bone-tired, but I still said yes.

WE DIDN'T TALK as I drove my mother to her halfway house. I didn't ask her what had happened. When we pulled into the uneven driveway, she thanked me. I hugged her goodbye, then waited as she made her way to the door, assuring her safe arrival inside by shining my headlights on her path. I watched her walk up the stairs, so slowly it almost looked like she was standing still.

At her follow-up appointment later that week, her cardiologist gave her a device to measure the rhythms of her heart. She was to wear the monitor around her neck all day and all night. Four days later, she called me and told me she didn't want it anymore.

"Come get this shit," she said angrily.

"What? Why?"

"It is too loud. It's uncomfortable. I can't sleep with it wrapped around my neck. Come get it," she pleaded.

The monitor was designed to send a message to the cardiologist and an ambulance if her heart stopped. It was meant to save her life. I ignored her second phone call that day, and I assume she slept with the hum for another night.

My mother called again the next day and begged me to take the device back. I knew that no matter how much I insisted she keep it, she would continue calling until I picked it up. She wanted me to return it because she had made an agreement with her doctor that if she wasn't using it, she would return it. She didn't want to use it anymore. I gave it some time, but eventually, drove over and put it in the trunk of my car. But I called my mother each day urging her to take it back. She refused each time and so, after a week, I returned it to the doctor's office.

I remember how tightly I held the little machine in my hand. Why couldn't she think of us and how worried we'd be about her and her heart?

THAT VERY NEXT weekend, my mother surprised me by showing up at Uncle Bubby's in a car I'd not seen before. She was in the passenger seat; an older redheaded woman with lots of fake jewelry was driving. I watched them from the kitchen window, my mother carrying a small tote bag and a gift bag tied with a pink balloon. I pushed the screen door open so they could make their way in.

"Happy birthday!" they shouted in unison, placing the bags on the torn yellow tablecloth on the round kitchen table.

All the surprises my mother had given me up until this point were related to her:

Surprise, Nikki, I'm in love with a new man.

Surprise, Nikki, I'm pregnant.

Surprise, Nikki, I'm in jail.

But this surprise was genuinely for me. "It's your birthday weekend, and we are going to have some cake," my mom said. "Also, I know you're going out to dinner tonight with the family, so I'll stay here and watch Jonathan."

I wasn't sure how to react. I felt so many different feelings: confused, glad to get a night off, though I'd planned to take Jonathan with me to celebrate, and unsure of what this meant for her relationship with Jonathan, with me. But I knew she was trying. While my mom babysat, I spent my twenty-fifth birthday at the Cheesecake Factory with my mom's younger brother, Uncle Main; his wife, Aunt Joann; and their two kids, Deja and Jared. Huddled together at dinner, we talked about my mother.

My uncle Main, a medium-height, dark-skinned man, was the most unpredictable human being I'd ever met. I am not sure if it was because of his impulsivity, his pent-up anger toward his siblings, or something else completely, but he was someone who could and would easily explode. The family would tease him about flying off the handle, but he'd brush it off. Even Main's own mother would mock him, saying that because he was born breech, "that's how he's always been—backwards."

It was hard to feel like I actually knew Main, or what made him tick. He was certainly someone who would speak his mind and share his opinions, and, like his sisters, he'd argue—or yell—to get his point across. His lips moistened with spit whenever he argued, his sentences often starting with "What the hell" or "Fuck you." He had a tendency to not think through what he said before he said it, whether he was talking to a boss, a friend, his parents, or me.

I'd always hoped to get to a place where Uncle Main would share his childhood with me, explain his volatility, help me understand who he was. He did tell me how bad he felt because Nanny and Poppy had kicked him out of the house at fifteen years old, that he had been a teenager who found it hard to simmer down after a heated argument, that he would take everything to the next level.

"You're going to have a heart attack because you're so angry," I cautioned. "Why don't you calm down?"

He shrugged off my question.

Despite the fact that he was married and had kids, I don't think Uncle Main was truly attached to anyone. I never saw him googly-eyed over his wife or particularly nurturing with his children. He'd met Aunt Jo, as I called her, when he was a senior in high school, and so they'd been together forever. I never saw him be sentimental about anything. He and Aunt Jo had a small apartment about thirty minutes from Uncle Bubby's house.

Today, Uncle Main had plenty to say about my mother. "It's fucked-up what she did to you," Uncle Main declared in his thick Long Island accent. "I mean c'mon, a grown-ass woman, and she keeps making the same mistakes. What's wrong with her?"

After our meal, a slice of chocolate cake with a single candle ceremoniously arrived at the table, and everyone joined in to sing "Happy Birthday" to me.

"Know that I'll always be here for you," Uncle Main told me. "Just call. Whateva you need."

On my drive home that night, I felt grateful to be celebrated, and I allowed myself a birthday wish. Maybe I *could* have that house that I dreamed of for Jonathan and me. And maybe it wouldn't be just me and him forever. Maybe lasting love would come into my life, a relationship that could help me build the family I always wanted.

WHEN I GOT back to Uncle Bubby's after dinner, I was prepared to creep up the stairs to my bedroom, expecting to see my mother there with Jonathan. Instead, she was sitting on the couch in the living room. She seemed content, and she was eager to hear about my evening.

"How was the night? How was Jonathan?" I asked her.

"He was good, and all went well. I fed him and bathed him, talked to Uncle Bubby, and then I stayed up for you."

"Let's go to bed then. I'm tired," I said.

"You go on up. I'll sleep here on the couch," she said.

"Mom, you can sleep with me. The bed is big enough."

"No, I'll be fine here," she said.

I kissed her, thanked her, and went to bed. This was the Lisa that her family loved—the one who would give them the shirt off her back. This was the Lisa I had long wanted in my life but had rarely witnessed. Though sometimes I'd seen glimpses.

Over the years, when my mom had a reprieve from her addictions, she had taken jobs styling hair, and she would do her sisters' hair when they asked, and she always did mine. She had also worked intermittently as a home health aide, and she was good at it. She had patience for older people, a strong stomach to handle changing adult diapers and wiping drool from faces. She saw the light that beamed from their hearts, and touched their souls in ways that gave them a twinkle in their eyes. Maybe she knew what it felt like to have no one listen to her or understand her, like so many of her clients experienced. The Lisa who stayed up the night of my twenty-fifth birthday dinner to ensure that I made it home safely, to hear about my evening, was the Lisa I prayed would hang around more.

WHILE LIVING AT Uncle Bubby's, I started a new job working with people with traumatic brain injuries. I'd keep them company, drive them to and from their doctor's appointments, and check in to see if I could help with anything. It wasn't what I had intended to do after graduation, but it helped me pay the bills. Jonathan was in a day care with caring people who gave me confidence that he was safe in my absence.

On Thursday, April 5, a few weeks after my mother had come to Uncle Bubby's bearing gifts, she called me at work asking for a favor: "Mama, can you stop and get my mail from Lady's house? I am going to take a nap, so call me before you come, okay?" Her voice sounded strained, almost like she'd been crying.

I asked if she was okay, and she said she was. I thought nothing more of it and promised her I'd call when I was on my way.

After work, I picked up Jonathan from day care and was putting him in the car seat when my phone rang. It was my mother's friend. She was sobbing and sounded really scared.

"There's a sheriff here at your mom's house, and he wants to talk to you," she told me.

I held my breath and waited as the sheriff was handed the phone.

"Your mother is a recovering addict, correct?"

"Yes, crack cocaine."

"Does your mother have any reason to harm herself?"

"No, she would never."

The truth was, my mother had many reasons to harm herself, too many to list. I was eerily calm with the sheriff, but my body was tense and I was starting to sweat.

"Do you know how to get to Brookhaven Memorial Hospital?" he asked.

"Yes."

"Can you meet the ambulance there?"

"Now?"

"The ambulance will meet you there."

Somehow, I knew as soon as I ended the call that my mother was dead.

A WHITE HOSPITAL blanket covered her lower body. Her face, arms, and feet remained exposed, her fingertips a light shade of blue. Her body was cold, her chest still, her soul gone. Seeing her there, I realized I knew very little about the woman I called Mom. Now, I would never know. Taking care of my mother, being available to her when she needed me—this had been my role in her life—and now the job had been taken away. I felt lost.

I called my grandmother from the hospital to give her the news. As I dialed, I was numb all over. I was in shock, unsure of what to do or where to go next. Nanny screamed, over and over and over again, and then one last time before it sounded like she'd fallen to the floor. Then my grandfather came on and asked me to tell him exactly what happened. I replayed for him what I knew. I told him the questions the cop had asked me over the phone, described my mother's lifeless body, and reported what I saw and what I knew. Eventually, the coroner's report would conclude that the cause of death was natural: arteriosclerotic and hypertensive heart disease.

My mother had her first heart attack at the age of twenty-eight, just after she gave birth to her second child, my brother Danny. Afterward, her heart was so weak that the cardiologist told her to dig herself a hole in the ground the next time she got the urge to smoke cocaine.

An autopsy could assess her cardiac condition and how much she had abused her heart—her drug use, her unhealthy food intake, her habit of smoking a few packs of Newport 100s a week—but it couldn't reveal how emotionally fragile and wholly defeated she was. My mother's heart could not endure the tangled stressors of abusive men, failed relationships, custody battles. It could not endure the confused emotions her absence caused in her children. Her heart was weakened with each court paper filed, each new curfew in a rehab facility, each click of handcuffs placed on her wrists.

My mother died at the age of forty-two while still on parole. She died in a halfway house with strangers, in a borrowed bed, recovering from an addiction, four months after giving birth to her fourth child. When I cleaned up her belongings, I found fresh notes in her Bible, almost as if she knew her last days were before her.

WHEN I ARRIVED at Galilee Church of God in Christ, it looked so small from the outside, its white pillars greeting me before I heard any voices. I walked slower than usual up the stairs and worked hard not to make eye contact with anyone as I entered the building. I did not have a lifetime with my mother, she did not die of old age, and she was never a mother figure in my life. In so many ways, she was a ghost when she was alive, and now she was a ghost of my past. I didn't want to look anyone in the face or hear what they had to say. I didn't know how to accept condolences for something that—it was hard to admit but true—had brought me a measure of relief.

The room where the wake took place felt dark and small, and smelled of cigarettes and too much perfume. It was filled with my mother's fellow addicts, some crying, some staring back at me with tortured looks on their faces. I walked around the periphery, finding my way to the front row, and sat down to take on my role as a daughter about to say goodbye to her mother— not over the phone or from behind a plexiglass window in jail, but for good.

Diana, a friend from college, had come to stay with me when

she heard my mother had died. At the ceremony, we sat so close to each other our shoulders touched, and from time to time she would put her arm around me. I had known Diana for five years. She was my constant, and I was hers. We shared our hopes and dreams. We shared the burdens of being the eldest child in both of our families. As a Mexican American, she told me what it was like to grow up in an immigrant family, and how her journey to Bard wasn't easy. In college, I admired her for how hard she worked, both in the classroom and on campus, putting herself through school and figuring out how to pay for it on her own.

Diana's strength and friendship steeled me when it was time for me to speak. I looked to her first as I stood next to my mother's open casket. "Do not wait to tell your loved ones you love them," I said. "You must leave here today and let them know how you feel, because tomorrow is not promised."

My speech went on much longer than I'd intended, the words pouring out of me like a broken faucet, like they would from a grieving daughter with regrets. I'm not even sure I believed them.

Even though my mother said she loved me often, I had difficulty saying it back. I was too angry. My mother was supposed to be the one who put Band-Aids on my wounds, the person who fed me chicken soup when I was sick, the one who told me how to mend a broken heart. Instead, I had taken care of her, and now she was gone.

THE NEXT DAY, I packed a rented minivan and drove with Jonathan, my sister's father, my great-uncle, my cousin Tiffany, and her two children to Virginia, where Nanny and Poppy lived.

My grandmother had decided that my mother would be buried at a cemetery near their house and that their minister would give the sermon.

"I never got the chance to meet Lisa, but I know she was loved and is in a better place," he said. "Her soul is at rest."

The sermon didn't move me. It didn't provide closure or hope, and I didn't feel God in the words the preacher offered.

Afterward, we walked one by one out of the church, and rain began to fall. As we made our way to my mother's gravesite, I could hear my aunt She-She's cries as she said goodbye to her older sister. I saw the subdued tears of my cousin Natasha. I saw Uncle Bob, all six feet of him, his dark sunglasses covering up his pain.

I sat in silence, staring at my mother's casket.

Jonathan's father, Karl, didn't attend the funeral in Virginia that day. He had shown up drunk at the wake in Riverhead, held up by two women. I'd only known who he was after Aunt Lady pointed him out to me. But Karl did stay in contact with me after my mother's death. I can't be certain whether his attempts to connect with me were for his son's sake or because of some heavy remorse that made him reconsider his position in our lives. Maybe they were the same thing.

As my mother left this world, her body buried in the red Virginia dirt, a new burden grew. My mother left me with dark shadows that would haunt me. Karl would soon come to dominate my life.

PART TWO

7

———

"ARE YOU READY for this?"

Twelve days after burying my mother, I was in family court alongside a social worker who'd visited us at Uncle Bubby's house. Before we entered the courtroom, she'd stopped and asked me that question—the same question she'd asked me twice before.

My answer came quickly and easily. "Yes, I am."

The court appearance was short. It was more of a formality— the state's need to check off whatever empty boxes were left. Lack of any criminal record was proof enough that I would not catch a DUI or go on some drug binge when parenthood became too stressful. They knew Jonathan was safe in my care and that my mother's presence could no longer put him in imminent danger. We moved from "temporary custody" to a whole new world of "residential custody," meaning I would be responsible for all of Jonathan's physical and emotional needs. The job description was permanent and clearly defined. Even if I had played the role for over four months by then, I was now no longer a stand-in. I was Jonathan's mother.

The next month, I was driving on the same expressway I had been on the day I went to meet Jonathan for the very first time. Only today I was headed in the opposite direction, driving Karl to take the paternity test he had requested before my mother died. He'd asked me to drive because his license was suspended.

My mother had thought that the paternity request was Karl's attempt to hold up the process of making child support payments. I kept thinking about her hunch now. Why was he contesting that he was the father? Was he trying to hurt my mother by insinuating that she was untrustworthy, that she slept around? Did her death make him doubtful about his connection to Jonathan?

Even with the air-conditioning blasting, it felt like I was suffocating—my mouth dry and my anxiety rising by the minute. The palms of my hands began to sweat as I gripped the steering wheel tighter. Karl sat next to me, skinny, average height, fine features, his skin as dark as night. From time to time, I glanced at Jonathan through the rearview mirror, curious as to what he was feeling or thinking or sensed.

When we arrived at the testing site it was—like so many other places I was forced to be—impersonal and bureaucratic. The staff were robotic, void of emotion and hesitant to make eye contact. But at least it was fast. A quick swab of Jonathan's cheek and then Karl's, and we were done.

As we walked down the stairs from the second floor, out to

the lobby, and into the parking lot, I could hear in my head the voices of the women in my family—my mother's the loudest.

From my mother:

Who the fuck do you think I was cheating on you with—huh, Karl? He is yours. I'll be damned if I don't make sure you don't see him. Please! Thinking he's not yours.

And from Aunt Lady:

You know damn well, Karl, that this baby is yours. Get off your shit. You know that you had sex, and now you're running from the responsibility of this baby 'cause you don't want to pay child support. You know who you are, what you did, and that you're just making everyone go through this. Don't ruin another life.

I'd always wondered where the women in my family got their strong voices, how they learned to be so assertive and direct, leaving zero room for anyone to question what they meant or what their needs were. I wanted to be like them in this moment, to shout out loud the words I'd heard my mother and my aunt say, as if they were standing right there with me. I wanted to shout at Karl that I didn't want him involved in Jonathan's life, to please go away and never bother us again.

Instead, I strapped Jonathan into his car seat and opened the driver's-side door.

"Well, that's done," I said. "And now we wait."

A WEEK BEFORE the paternity test, I had visited Aunt Eva, who lived in the same town as Uncle Bubby, not far from his house. I'd been stopping by regularly since Jonathan was a tiny infant.

A large woman with belly rolls and almost-white hair, Aunt Eva was my grandmother's sister-in-law from her first marriage. Aunt Eva had been fond of my mother, and the two had kept in touch. It was Aunt Eva who had provided Jonathan's playpen.

"What's that baby gonna sleep in, Nikkya?" she'd asked before presenting us with the thoughtful gift.

Part of me carried a little fear of Aunt Eva, maybe because of how she asked questions in a stern and sometimes accusatory way. Maybe it was because she was an elder, or perhaps because she held my grandmother's ear too close, whether it was to vent about her own drug-addicted son or to share the town gossip.

Just as assertive as the women on my grandmother's side of the family, Aunt Eva didn't beat around the bush. She got straight to the point. "You gonna let him call you Mama, ain't cha?" Aunt Eva asked, leaning over the island in the middle of her kitchen, the afternoon sun shining through the skylight and onto her face. It magnified her beautiful skin, which was void of wrinkles or marks.

Her question caught me off guard. I held Jonathan closer, let my nose rest in the crook of his neck. I closed my eyes and considered it. It was a difficult question. My mother was gone from this earth, but she was his birth mother. I stalled.

"Well, I am waiting," Eva prompted. "Everybody needs somebody to call Mama. Lord knows he will need that. Won't cha baby?" She rubbed Jonathan's plump cheek, and he buried his face deeper into my neck.

I could feel his baby softness, smell his wonderful baby smell. It was pure bliss, comforting in a way I had never experienced before. I peeked down at him to see his response to her touch and caught his eyes as they followed Aunt Eva around the island, sizing her up.

"I've thought about it, but I am not sure," I confessed. I felt my heart beat a little faster.

"What's there to think about? You gonna take him back to da hospital? Return him?" she said. And before I could respond, she answered for me. "No, you ain't. So let him call you Mama. You had someone to call Mama, didn't cha?"

She wasn't wrong. I'd had Lisa to call Mama, and Nanny to fulfill the role. My mind raced, trying to think of the best way to put an end to this line of questioning. I knew I was the one who was able to give him what my mother could never give me: stability. Though she'd tried while she was alive, she could not regain custody of Jonathan. He would never be able to call *her* Mama.

"I will think about it some more, Aunt Eva. I'll let you know what I decide. Maybe he will decide for me."

THE REALITY NOW was that my mother was dead. I was Jonathan's only mama, and he was my sole responsibility—at least until we knew what Karl's next move was. Before Jonathan was able to form his first words, I wanted to figure out this name thing.

I also wanted to ensure that I could be a single mom who was actually present. I didn't want to miss my son taking his first step or losing his first tooth. In order to be who Jonathan needed me to be, I had to find a new job, one that paid more than the brain injury center but also one that was flexible enough for me to be there for him.

Though interviewing and taking care of four-month-old Jonathan was exhausting, I eventually managed to get a job as a teacher's assistant at a day care in town. I'd be working with one- and two-year-olds. I found pride in the work, and an opportunity to give back to the community I was now a part of. And while I was keeping other people's kids safe, Jonathan was also safe—I was able to register him at the day care, so I knew exactly where he was at any moment of the day. That gave me peace of mind and prevented my worry about him from eating me alive.

When we weren't at the day care, Jonathan and I would spend time at the ocean, the water a solace. My feelings about being back home, on Long Island, without any real idea of when we'd be able to leave, were complicated, like everything else. My memories of the place were mixed up with my struggles with my mother and the demons that followed her. I'd lived on Long Island from the time I was born until I was five years old. Just after I started kindergarten, Nanny and Poppy decided to move us to Pennsylvania, where we lived until I was twelve. My younger aunts, She-She and Kendra, moved with us, as they often traveled as a pair.

Aunt Kendra was the listener—careful not to jump in too quickly to support one sibling over another, not assertive enough to call people out when they were wrong. Incredibly easy-going, she had the memory of an elephant. Aunt Kendra and Aunt She-She were inseparable. In high school, they did everything together, including traveling to Italy for a class trip. Aunt

She-She was the baby of the family—her siblings considered her the golden child, and she was, in essence, many things they were not. She graduated from high school and then college—she was still in college, not yet married to Steve, when she moved with us to Pennsylvania—and she had a vision for her life. She wanted to be a singer and styled her hair short, à la Whitney Houston. Her naturally thin frame bolstered the comparison. She even had a job at Sony Records.

Growing up, I looked up to She-She and admired her for both her beauty and her ambition. She had lots of friends, and she was skinny—both things I wanted to be. And I wanted to be the apple of my mother's eye, like She-She seemed to be for Nanny. In some ways, She-She tried to parent me, giving me advice and helping me with my history and English homework. She showed me a tender kind of love—I guess the kind of love and care that aunties tend to show.

Aunt Kendra never married or had kids of her own, nor did she have an idea of where she saw her career path going. One of her very first jobs was working at McDonald's—she stayed long enough to become manager before going to Wendy's and moving up there, too. I remember that she used to sneak me vanilla ice cream cones from those fast-food chains.

For a while, Kendra had been the neighborhood babysitter. By the time I graduated from high school, she was working as a teacher's assistant at a school for kids with special needs. When she spoke about the kids she cared for and taught, her big dark-brown eyes lit up with joy, her wide smile revealed the gap between her two front teeth, and her cheekbones rose so high that I could see a dimple or two. Kendra was and is very compassionate.

During my first year in middle school, my grandparents were forced out of our Pennsylvania home due to foreclosure. We moved back to New York, where we rented a house and then a condo, before my grandparents finally settled in Virginia, where my grandmother was originally from. During my freshman year of high school, I briefly lived in Virginia with my grandmother, but it felt like I didn't belong in my classes or with the student body. It was a massive school, and I got lost. That's when I moved to Aunt Lady's house. With all the back-and-forth from state to state, I never felt like home was anywhere in particular. I didn't want to repeat that pattern with Jonathan. I wanted to choose differently for him.

TEN DAYS AFTER the paternity test, and two months after my mother died, I was back in family court, only this time with Karl beside me, both of us standing in front of the same judge who had granted me residential custody. Karl had been newly confirmed as Jonathan's father, and he had petitioned for joint custody. This appearance was a formality, a detail to be entered into the record so that another court date would be set to either stick with the current decision (I would maintain sole residential custody) or change it (Karl and I would share joint custody).

It was my second time in court, and I was determined to speak straight from my heart, loud enough for strangers to hear, and to leverage some of the emotions still raw from having to bury my mother. "It's in Jonathan's best interest to remain with me, as I can provide a stable, loving, and understanding home for him," I said. My voice was strong, but inside I was shaking. "He is the last child of my mother's, and it is what she wanted—for us to stay together as a family."

The judge decided not to make any changes to the current agreement. Residential custody would remain with me. Karl did not contest. Everything would remain as it had been. At least for now.

I thought of Karl being drunk at my mother's wake. I thought of how he had cheated on his wife with my mother. I thought of the inconsiderate way he spoke to her when she was alive, dismissing her words with ease.

Before I'd ever met any of the men in my mother's life, she had a way of "introducing" them, by telling me stories about them—hoping that by sharing tidbits and offering crumbs of their courtship it would endear them to me. It didn't. I never liked any of the people my mother dated. Maybe it wasn't really the men, but instead the way my mother lost herself in their world.

She shared with me once that she often met Karl, for what she considered a date, at the aquarium where he worked as a custodian. "We hold hands and walk around and look at all the fish. Girl, he knows so much about those damn fish," she said. "He told me he's gonna leave that wife of his. She knows he's not happy. And he always has money. He makes sure I don't go without either."

To her, that meant something. To me, it meant nothing. But it did make me wonder if Karl was different from my selfish father, who always seemed to prefer Jack Daniel's to the company of other human beings. I wondered if perhaps the motivation behind Karl's appeal for custody was really a desire for some last bit of control over my mother—which he could gain by having control over me and Jonathan. He had been a ghost, and now he was here, haunting us with his unfinished business.

When we left the court, he barely looked at us.

THAT SUMMER, AFTER the paternity test results were in, Karl started calling to ask me to bring Jonathan to his work for a quick visit. Even though it would have been entirely reasonable, I couldn't summon the courage to ask him to visit our house instead. Maybe he still didn't have a license—I don't know—but I was afraid to suggest he get someone to drive him to Uncle Bubby's if he wanted to see his son. Would he hear it as a demand and petition me again in court for something more? Would he seek sole custody of Jonathan?

I said yes every time Karl made the unfair demand. It felt like a complete waste of my time—and his—but if this was what I had to do to keep Jonathan with me exclusively, I was willing. He would come out of his workplace, peek in at Jonathan in his car seat, and say hello. Karl never asked any questions about his son. He didn't ask if Jonathan was eating solid foods, or crawling, or sleeping through the night. His questions were always about me. Once, he even asked me to go out to dinner with him alone.

"I know you've been working hard with Jonathan. Let me take you out."

He had a particular tone, one that I perceived as him asking me on a *date*.

"No, thank you," I said, holding back vomit. Karl was incapable of showing any interest in his son—and now he wanted me to leave Jonathan behind and go out with him?

I wanted Jonathan to know his father because I didn't want him to ask questions when he got older about why he never saw him. But Jonathan was getting nothing out of the visits—no bonding, no hugs, no affection, no financial support. I was torn. Was my taking him to see his father any time Karl called necessary, especially when Karl offered so little?

Karl had four older kids, some of whom were in and out of jail. Karl barely talked about them to me. He seemed to have had an out-of-sight, out-of-mind kind of parenting style. He knew how to be polite when it was required but lacked emotional intelligence. In fact, as far as I could tell he had only three emotions: anger, excitement, and detachment. I'd recognized similar struggles in others with addiction issues. Which one would show up when was hard to predict.

I am sure my mother had mental health issues that went undiagnosed, ones she self-medicated with crack cocaine and the occasional rum and Coke. I suppose she was drawn to Karl because he had similar struggles. Later, when Jonathan would be given various diagnoses—attention deficit hyperactivity disorder, anxiety disorder, and on the autism spectrum—I knew those burdens were an inheritance.

I NEEDED A plan. I didn't want to stay on Long Island one second longer than I had to, but I didn't understand whether or not we could legally move away from Karl. I was also too exhausted to figure out how to move out of Uncle Bubby's house and didn't want to add another battle to the field we were already fighting on.

At night, I would watch Jonathan's chest rise and fall, and I would pray to God to tell us where we were meant to go. While I strained to understand some of God's plans for my life—like why I was born into the family I was or why I was given an absent mother and a father who never wanted me—I felt I had been gifted Jonathan for a reason. Somewhere buried deep down, I believed in God, and I knew God had trust in me, even though I felt lost.

Karl's unsteadiness jeopardized us all. He had accepted the idea of his new son while Jonathan was in utero, but once he was a living, breathing being among us, Karl claimed he was not Jonathan's father. Now he wanted to see his son, but I saw no evidence that he was inclined to build a relationship with him or even take him to the bathroom. He was always inconsistent. With so much out of my control, I began to take more comfort from my faith and spirituality.

Some people think that because I am queer, there is no way I could have a relationship with God. When I was a kid, I hated going to church. My grandparents' roles as deacon and usher at our Baptist church meant I had to sit for hours listening to long sermons, wondering if I'd ever know the kind of faith my grandparents knew. But now, whenever I feel weak and worried, questioning if I've made the right decisions for Jonathan, I need God to hear my prayers, to forgive me for being so inconsistent in my past practice, and to help me find the strength to face whatever is around the corner.

8

WITH ALL THE pressures of motherhood and work, I rarely came up for air. One day in July of 2007, Lady offered to babysit so I could go to an afternoon hair appointment.

"I will watch Jonathan, and you go and get your hair done," she insisted.

I went to the same hair salon Lady and Natasha visited regularly. Sitting in the chair, I felt a little strange to be so pampered. But it was definitely something a girl could get used to. I ended up making a standing appointment for every four weeks. Nanny and Poppy paid for the indulgence.

It was not unusual for my grandparents to come to my rescue—they'd been doing it my whole life. Both on their second marriage, they didn't have any biological children together, and I was the baby they raised as partners. Poppy was my step-grandfather, but my skin was just as dark as his, he was short, just like me, and our facial features resembled each other—so much so that strangers often mistook us for biological father and daughter. He never corrected them, because in so very many ways I was his. Nanny and Poppy never allowed me to call them Mom and Dad, out of respect for my parents, but they were closest to the real thing.

I came to look forward to my monthly conversations with my new hairstylist, Perry. His fingers massaging my scalp, my body melting into the lush white leather chair, he revived my forgotten dreams along with my hair. I'd close my eyes and remember my mother doing my hair, one of the few memories I have of her being maternal. I'd sit between her legs, her knees pressed hard against my shoulders to hold me steady. She would wrap her thumb and index finger around my hair, pulling my scalp so tight that my eyes would burn. She'd breathe heavily, in part due to her being overweight, and in part due to her cigarette smoking and asthma. She'd weave in dark-brown synthetic hair, giving me long braids to welcome the new school year.

Perry had known my mother, so I was able to let my guard down a little bit and talk about her. I'd tell him about all the times she would light up a family gathering with her imitations of other family members, or how she'd get that deep belly laugh after a few too many Budweisers.

"Your mama was always makin' somebody laugh," Perry reminisced. "Thinkin' she could sang, girl."

The two of us laughed. My mother loved to sing, but she had a particular talent for turning a perfectly good tune into what sounded like a cat fight in the middle of the night. One of her favorites was Mary J. Blige's "Not Gon' Cry," and whenever it came on the radio, no matter where she was, she would belt out the chorus, hand motions all over the place, eyes closed as if she were standing at a microphone in front of thousands at Madison Square Garden.

No, I'm not gon' cry.

I would imagine she was singing the song lines to all the men who broke her heart over the years.

At some point, I shared with Perry that I was a lesbian. His mouth dropped open. He was clearly shocked, especially given how religious my grandparents were. I held my breath waiting for him to speak—I valued Perry's advice as much as I did his cutting the split ends off my hair. He was a gay man with lived experience in the community.

"I know Ms. Kitty got somethin' to say about that, huh?" he said, referring to my grandmother.

Perry understood that Nanny's religious views and Southern upbringing could mean she'd be resistant to accepting my sexuality.

Over the years, I'd introduced Nanny to some of the women I'd dated, but she still hung on to the hope—the belief—that I would find a nice young man. And anyway, there was no one serious until Kate came along. Nanny had been kind and respectful to all my friends, unsure of which girl I'd introduced her to was actually a girlfriend or just a girl I'd befriended. Kate was the first girl I brought home and introduced as my girlfriend. With Kate, I knew Nanny was against our relationship—but it wasn't really about sexuality. "You're going to have trouble when you're with someone outside of your race," she said. She was never outwardly rude to Kate, but generally lukewarm. It wasn't until

Nanny realized I wanted to marry Kate that she understood that my queerness was here to stay.

Once my secret was out with Perry, he'd have something to say about my nonexistent love life at every hair appointment. "When are you going to let somebody love you?" he would ask. "You can't just be someone's mama forever. You need to get back out there, girl."

My decision to become Jonathan's guardian was the straw that broke the camel's back for Kate and me. It was too much for us to navigate together, but in February of 2007 we still had not officially ended things. Jonathan and I were living at Lady's, my mother was in rehab, and it was time.

Uncle Bob, Natasha's father, agreed to drive me and Jonathan up to Erie, Pennsylvania, where Kate was going to school, to help me pack up my belongings from her apartment and bring them home. It'd been at least three months since Kate and I had seen each other, although with everything going on in my life it felt more like years. Kate and I ended up sleeping next to each other that night in her loft area. Jonathan slept in the bed with me. Bob was on the couch below.

I ran my hand over Kate's forearm in the dark and allowed my lips to meet hers, hoping to feel something in that moment between us that would convince me I was wrong, that I should fight for what we had. There was nothing. There was no spark. There were no butterflies. I said to her, "You don't have to be anyone's mother. You have a life to live. Live that life." When we woke up early the next morning, I did not cry. She did. We both knew this was it.

The car was packed, we hugged one last time, and when the door to Uncle Bob's black Tahoe closed, I felt content. I had hoped that things could have been different between me and Kate. I loved her, but we had too many personal hills to climb. Plus, I chose Jonathan over our relationship. I knew it was right for Kate and it was right for Jonathan and me, but sometimes I missed her. I said so to Perry now.

"Where she at? She ain't here. So no pining away for her," he said as he tapped his brush. "Time to get it moving."

I let out a long sigh.

"And, chile, you need someone who has better credit than you."

We both laughed loudly as he placed his shearing scissors back in the khaki-colored tool belt at his waist.

In his mirror, my high cheekbones, crooked smile, and dark skin looked different, unfamiliar even to me. I felt more confident than I had in many months. With one last spin in Perry's white chair, I was out the door and ready for the world, my dark-brown hair bone-straight and flying in the summer night's air.

TRUTH IS, I had already started thinking about dating before Perry urged me to get back out there. I'd started thinking about it before my mom died. Besides the lack of free time in my life, though, I wasn't sure I could handle it. I feared anyone who knew my full story would run the other way—and fast. How could I explain on a first date what standing in line for WIC vouchers felt like? Or that my mother was addicted to crack? Or that I wanted legal custody of my half brother? Or that my mother had four kids with four different men?

Because I had enough complications in my life already, I needed an uncomplicated relationship. I needed a person who would see me for me, who would help me without asking, who would take care of me. That was a tall order, I knew, especially when I was still coming to terms with the fact that I needed to ask for any help at all.

But now with that push from Perry, I was willing to dip my feet in the water. In my borrowed room with its aging wood-panel walls, while Jonathan napped in his little playpen, I connected to the internet. My search included phrases like *dating sites for lesbians* and *single lesbians with children*. I clicked on TangoWire, the first website that popped up, and created a user-name and password. With the hum of my dial-up modem and the squeak of the old bed, I held my breath in anticipation of my search results.

9

———

I READ THE words *believer, faith,* and *honesty* in her profile while I waited for the website to finish loading her photo. The top part emerged before the bottom, and her dark curly hair immediately caught my eye. Next came the speckled brown eyeglasses resting on her nose, and then the warmest, most open smile I'd ever seen. I wondered who was behind the camera and what they had done to elicit the pure joy that was all over her face. Her cheeks were round, and her caramel skin crystal clear, not a mole or a pimple in sight. Was she Latina? Indian? I read on, discovering she was Sri Lankan, from a place I'd never heard of. She taught sixth grade in the South Bronx. Her big brown eyes seemed to be looking right into mine, even through her glasses and my screen.

Jonathan cried out, and luckily, with one gentle pat on his back, he went back to sleep.

I continued my search, clicking through a few other profiles, just in case she was not "the one," but I kept coming back to her page. Her name was Dinushka. Her smile was what kept me returning. There was something so honest and innocent, so warm about the way her lips, slightly parted, showed her perfectly white teeth. I just sensed her goodness and openness. I practiced saying her name out loud in my bedroom. I sent a smiley-face emoji in hopes she'd understand that I wanted to talk to her and waited only a few hours before her response came in. From there, we started writing to each other every day as if we were old friends picking up an old conversation. Her words were authentic and flowed easily. She knew who she was. She spoke from her heart about her values and life.

I learned that Dinushka and her family immigrated to the United States from Sri Lanka when she was around five years old and her brother was ten. Her parents moved to Queens first before deciding to make Connecticut their home. She'd become a teacher because she loved children, but also because her South Asian parents thought that it would be a stable profession with good benefits. Ultimately, though, she wanted a religious life, to study theology and become a lay minister in the Catholic Church.

Though I couldn't connect with her calling, the pressures I felt from my family were not dissimilar to those she felt from her own. "You will never get anywhere in this world if you don't have a degree," my grandfather would say. For my grandparents, an education meant better pay, job security, and that you'd "made it."

My mother had dropped out of high school, and we never talked about academics or what I was learning in school. She once told me she had loved lunch and recess and not much else.

Even though Dinushka was unsure about whether she would continue teaching, I loved that she valued education as much as I did.

The year before she started her current job at a charter school, she'd traveled alone through Egypt, Portugal, France, and Spain. Dinushka's courage to do so and her sense of adventure was exciting to me. Her parents both worked for the United Nations and were travelers themselves. Every other summer, they would plan a trip to a different country for the four of them before they returned to Sri Lanka to visit family. They wanted their kids to see the world. I had never been outside the country, except for a winter break trip to Mexico my sophomore year of college. I almost felt ashamed of my lack of worldliness.

At first, I was selective about how much I shared with Dinushka. I told her that my mother had recently died and that I was taking care of my brother, but I feared that telling her more than that too soon would push her away. On the other hand, I also worried that telling her too little wouldn't paint an honest picture of who I was. Soon, I felt comfortable enough to open up a bit about my unusual situation.

It turned out it was easier to explain my mother's addiction and the time she spent in jail—these experiences showed my mother's poor judgment and were far removed from me—than to admit how little time I'd actually spent with her growing up and how much of my life I'd spent chasing after a woman I could never catch, someone to whom I was devoted but who could not return that commitment. I told Dinushka enough to help her understand why I was afraid of losing someone I cared about.

But I still wanted to be cautious, because we hadn't yet had a date and I didn't know whether this would even work out.

What I did know was that she was like no other person I'd ever met.

I'D TRIED FOR a long time to be "normal." I wanted to be like all the other girls my age—girls who liked boys—but in eighth grade I became completely smitten with my classmate Chloe, who would become my first girlfriend.

Chloe was tall, skinny, and white, with dark-brown, shoulder-length hair, which she kept in a low ponytail. She played a sport every season—soccer, volleyball, and basketball—and between her athletics schedule and academics, she didn't have much time for hanging out. During basketball season, I sat courtside as her team's scorekeeper. I had no interest in the game, or sports in general, but I wanted to be close to Chloe. As the season went on, I learned who was the point guard, what three-point shots were, and what the difference was between offense and defense. At every game, I'd hear my aunt Lady screaming "Big D!" She was there supporting Natasha, who was also on the team.

Chloe was popular, funny, and a good listener. At first, I was uncertain of what I was feeling for her. I knew it wasn't just "I have a new best friend" but something more, but I didn't have a name for it. I could be open with her in ways that I couldn't be with others. It felt safe to tell her about my mother. She didn't judge me.

One night, while at a sleepover at Chloe's house, we finally confessed that we had feelings for each other and shared a soft and gentle first kiss. As our eighth-grade year progressed, we told no one about our relationship. In our hearts, we knew we were meant to be together. It was classic puppy love, the kind that middle school dreams are made of.

As I rushed out of the house to head to school one morning, I accidentally dropped a love note I'd written to Chloe the night before. In it, I'd shared my excitement: *I can't wait to sleep over at your house this weekend. We can stay up all night and talk, and you know what else! I don't want to keep what we have a secret.*

I signed off with *X*'s and *O*'s.

I had planned on passing the note to her during first period, but instead Nanny found it, read it, and was waiting for me when I got home from school.

"God will judge you," she told me. "This is not what you should be doing. This is against the Bible. Nikki, you aren't that way."

But I *was* that way. I was not going to deny it, but I didn't confirm it, either. I said nothing. I didn't want to let my grandmother down. I believed then that being a gay person meant that I would bring her shame—and my mother had already brought her plenty of that.

I still planned to sleep over at Chloe's house, though, even if Nanny's silent treatment told me how angry she was. Poppy took me, and we drove the ten-minute trip without talking.

When we stopped in front of Chloe's house, the engine of his blue pickup truck rumbled as we idled. I lingered a little longer to see if he would say anything, whether he would acknowledge what we both knew. But there was no Sunday morning sermon from him like I'd gotten from Nanny. I opened the door.

"I'll be here tomorrow morning to pick you up. Let me know what time," was all he said, which I took as an indication that he loved me no matter what, even if he didn't understand.

I knew Nanny would need to tell somebody eventually and that the news of my infatuation would then spread like wildfire through my family. Though Natasha hadn't yet said anything, I was sure she suspected something, sure she had seen me at basketball games looking adoringly at Chloe. I didn't want Nanny or Natasha to be the one to announce this kind of news—that was for me to do.

One day when I got home from school, my aunt Kendra, my mother, and Natasha were all at the house, and I felt the time was right. I asked them to sit down, and then the floodgates opened, my truth pouring out of me.

"I don't like boys," I said.

"If you don't like boys, then who do you like?" Natasha asked.

"I like girls," I said.

There was collective shock, and then my mother broke the awkwardness.

"Mama, I love you and will always love you, no matter what," she said. "You're my daughter, and I'll be by your side forever. Now, this little Chloe betta' not break your heart—or else she will deal with me, you got it?"

My mother's swift acceptance at that moment, for which I was grateful, was not the reaction of most of my relatives, many of whom had homophobic views. I cringed every time I heard a family member calling someone a "dyke" or a "faggot" in con-versation. My aunts and uncles didn't know any better, didn't understand why that was hurtful, and I didn't yet have the cour-age to explain why the way they spoke was offensive. After I came out, I often felt guilty for not standing up for myself and my community, for not making them see that their words were akin to someone calling them a "nigger."

I also knew that many in my family held on to a hope that I would one day miraculously fall in love with a man and build my happily ever after with him. That was until they met Dinushka and saw that my happily ever after was with her.

I'D BEEN OUT to both friends and family when I met Dinushka. Most had come to terms with who I was, even if they didn't like it per se namely, my grandparents, Aunt She-She, Aunt Kendra, and Uncle Wayne. Dinushka had told only a small group of close friends, and her parents did not know she was gay. I understood. Being out is a scary prospect, especially when losing one's family is a very real possibility.

When Dinushka and I met in 2007, homosexuality was a crime in Sri Lanka. According to Human Rights Watch, if some-one was thought or found to be gay, they could be sentenced to jail. There is more hope today for equality for LGBTQI people in Sri Lanka, but there is still a very long way to go.

After Dinushka immigrated to the United States, her family returned home to Sri Lanka most summers, and as she began to acknowledge her sexuality those visits brought fear with them. Despite my own painful experiences when I came out at fifteen,

I had a privilege that Dinushka didn't yet have in her own home-land. And I was too naive to know then that the United States could also be a dangerous place for people like me and her.

FOR WEEKS, I looked forward to Dinushka's emails, exciting gifts after a long day of wiping little butts and noses at the day care. As soon as I got home, before I changed out of my work clothes, I opened my laptop and prayed that a message from her would appear. More often than not, it would be there—she was my oasis from grief and from the stress of being a single working mother.

Jonathan filled me with love as only a child can, but Dinushka, through our email conversations, was holding me and my current reality with a tenderness that I also badly needed. With each message, I began to tell her more and more about who I was, allowing her to see my fears, anxieties, hopes and dreams.

She, in turn, reassured me:

You are doing better than most, my love. You have chosen to love your baby brother as your own son, you took care of your mother when she needed you, you've chosen a job in which you help others, and in return, God will provide for you if you ask, and continue to give the best that is inside your heart. I am calm and relieved in my heart to have met you. I hope to soon watch cheesy television with you and eat mac and cheese with you and kiss you all over and hold your body to mine.

10

A MONTH AFTER our first email, Dinushka and I planned our first date. Jonathan was ten months old, and I still wasn't entirely comfortable leaving him with anyone other than my coworkers at the day care or close family members. Despite this, when my dear friend Lauren from my college days at Bard offered to babysit at her house, I agreed.

By then, Jonathan and I had been living at Uncle Bubby's for six months, but our clothes were still only half-unpacked. It was an unnerving way to live, even though I recognized that Jonathan and I were lucky to be Bubby's guests. As someone who had experienced trauma, I kept myself emotionally safe by always having an exit strategy at the start of every new situation, and in this case not fully unpacking was my way of being ready to leave quickly if necessary.

Now I searched for my favorite jeans in my mess of a suitcase, along with a short-sleeved green T-shirt. I applied my strawberry-flavored lip gloss and headed out to the car. I strapped

Jonathan into the back seat, along with his Pack 'n Play, hopped on the highway, and drove north, an hour and a half from Uncle Bubby's, to where Lauren lived with her wife. Lauren knew and loved Jonathan, and he was comfortable with her, and she recognized that it was important for me to get back out in the world and have some fun. I gave Jonathan a kiss and Lauren a thank-you pat, and off I went.

I wasn't the best at navigating while driving, so I left Long Island with ample time to get lost and still make it on time for lunch with Dinushka. On the way to the Bronx, anxiety set in: Was this the right thing to do? Should I be leaving Jonathan just to go on a date? My mother had always left me to search for drugs or love from a man. Was this the same? If Dinushka and I weren't compatible, then I would have left him for no reason at all.

Though it was only an hour away from where we lived, I'd rarely been to New York City—and I'd never driven into the city myself. I'd taken the train to pick my mother up from Bayview Correctional Facility, and in high school, my humanities class took a field trip to the Metropolitan Museum of Art. That was about the extent of my exposure to the city, and I didn't like the smell, the dirty streets, the loud noises, and the fast pace of it all.

I had to circle the block a few times to find a parking space near Dinushka's apartment, but the minute I got out of the car I found myself walking fast, adrenaline propelling me along the sidewalk like a real New Yorker.

Dinushka's place was on the first floor of a prewar building. I rang the buzzer and waited for what felt like an eternity. I gave my armpits one quick sniff and applied another coat of lip gloss. Just then, a person left the building, allowing me to sneak in. I only knew Dinushka's apartment number, the rest I had to navigate on my own. Whether I am walking or driving somewhere, unless I'm with someone with a good sense of direction, I get lost rather easily. Like magic, though, I found myself in front of her door. Feeling proud I had arrived, I took three deep breaths and knocked.

She opened the door with a small laugh. My smile was wide as we hugged briefly. We were finally meeting. Butterflies had taken up residence in my belly. She was even cuter in person.

"Come in! Come in!" she beckoned, waving her hands.

I immediately noticed how clean and tidy her studio apartment was, so different from the sad, lonely room Jonathan and I occupied at Bubby's. A little white desk and a wicker chair were flush against the far wall. On the futon that doubled as her bed, I sat as close to her as I possibly could. I hoped she wouldn't see me as too eager, but I wanted some physical connection, even if it was just a brush of her arm against mine.

I continued to survey the room and walked over to her bookshelf. She followed and then pulled out a brown leather photo album. It looked brand-new, but the photos inside told a different story. They were older photos of her family, mostly, and some of her friends, too.

"Do you miss Sri Lanka?" I asked.

"Sometimes I do. But it's illegal for me to be gay there, and the culture is very conservative. I never fully fit in."

"But you still have family there, right? So it must be hard."

"It is. But I am a Sri Lankan American, and I consider New York my home, too." She closed the well-worn album. "Are you ready for lunch?" she asked.

"I think so."

We stepped out onto the streets of New York and walked side by side up the steep subway stairs and onto an elevated platform. We didn't speak much on the train. We'd already shared a lot over email—or maybe we were testing how comfortable we'd be not saying a word. We ate at a restaurant in Lower Manhattan, where I ordered fried chicken with a side salad and she ordered a waffle topped with fresh strawberries and whipped cream. We had to almost shout to hear each other, and Dinushka's voice bellowed over the table, like a teacher trying to get the attention of her class. I watched her every move—from the way she gently nodded her head to acknowledge a point I'd made to the way her red Gap T-shirt revealed some of her cleavage. I felt both attracted to and comfortable with her.

I was hanging out with someone I really enjoyed. Just like it was on email, it was as if we were picking up an old conversation.

After we ate, Dinushka and I walked through the streets of Manhattan together. "I love living in New York," she said. "There is always something to do. On any given day, you can walk out of your apartment and attend a festival. Or run into friends. Or go to a museum."

"Isn't it too noisy? It smells awful."

"True," she said, "but you get used to it."

"I don't know if I ever could live in a city this big. I'm from the suburbs. I like to jump into my car and drive where I need to go."

We strolled without any idea of where we were headed or what we wanted to do, eventually ending up at the Angelika, an independent movie theater. On a whim, we decided to see the film playing there, *Two Days in Paris*. Dinushka bought the tickets, and I bought a large popcorn and Twizzlers from the concession stand. We stuffed ourselves into the narrow seats, our elbows touching on the armrest, so close I could feel the hairs on her arm.

I wanted to hold her hand in the darkness of the theater, to trace the lifeline on her palm as we laughed through the movie. Her laugh was a hearty roar, and each time I heard it, I caught myself looking around, checking to see if people were annoyed, but no one seemed to mind. I finished all the snacks myself, trying to settle the butterflies I was still intermittently experiencing.

When the movie ended, I prepared to part ways with her. I felt the pull to get back to Jonathan, but Dinushka suggested we walk and talk a little more. When I agreed, we took a quick subway ride to Central Park and happened upon an open-air bar. We'd spent all day together, but I knew I was still putting up a wall. A cranberry and vodka loosened me up enough to finally let it down. Dinushka's own mojito quelled her nervous banter and allowed her more philosophical side to come out, the one I already knew from our emails:

What makes certain people stay together, like my parents, for thirty years? she'd written. *What binds them, what's that*

connection that lasts, that grows, that keeps you constantly learn-
ing and moving everything in you? It's love—but how do you know
when that love is real and grounded?

"Why do you think some relationships last forever while others end so quickly?" I asked now.

"Well, my parents, they are in a love marriage. It wasn't
arranged," she said. "They don't always see eye to eye, but they
have the same values. I think that's what couples need."

"My grandparents' marriage is the second one for both of
them," I told her. "I am sure their common faith drew them
together."

"What about you? Do you think you'll find that person who
you just fall in love with and that's it, you'll know the marriage
will last?"

"I don't know," I said. "These days I don't think too much
about getting married. But I think about having kids all the
time."

Dinushka also didn't believe she would marry, but she definitely wanted a partner, someone to share her life with. She
talked about wanting to adopt at least one child. The truth was,
we were both unsure of what life held for us. We were queer
women of color, coming from conservative cultures, having to
carve out something new.

Dinushka and I found a spot underneath a huge oak tree and
settled in to finish our drinks. She shared some of the difficulties
she'd faced as a child, that she hadn't come from a perfect past
or a perfect family, as I had assumed. We talked about God, and
how her calling in life was a pastoral one. I shared my ups and

downs with faith and uncertainty, wondering where God was in my life, given all the hardship.

Our date had become the longest, most heartfelt one I'd ever been on.

Finally, I called Lauren to check on Jonathan. Did he eat? Did he cry? Did she change his diaper? What was he doing now? Was he scared?

Lauren assured me he was fine, but talking with her was a reality check: I would never find a woman to take both me and Jonathan. No one would be able to deal with the intense strain I had lived with for almost a year—from Jonathan coming into my life to burying my mom, from Karl's demands to my tenuous housing situation to my lack of funds even for groceries. This was my world, and though the date was going well, I needed to be clear-sighted.

With the last sip of my drink, I decided it was time to go home. I already felt guilty for leaving Jonathan for so long. But just before we were about to enter the subway, Dinushka grabbed my hand. "Will you spend the night with me?" she asked.

I was stunned, but then I felt a quiver throughout my body, from head to toe. A yes reverberated within me but never found its way out. We walked down the stairs to the train. And then, right there on the platform, Dinushka leaned in to kiss me just as, out of the corner of my eye, I caught a glimpse of a large rat scurrying on the track. I let out a squeal and backed away from her. I caught my breath.

"This will not be our first kiss, here, like this," I said.

Embarrassed, and I think relieved, Dinushka stepped back and we both waited for the train to arrive, saying nothing more. We sat quietly, arm to arm, on the blue subway seats as the train barreled down the tracks. Two stops from her apartment, Dinushka asked her question again.

"Will you spend the night with me? We can just sleep. Share a bed."

Our date had moved so fast and yet so slow. In fact, all our predate email exchanges made me feel like we had been on a date for the last thirty days. And now she wanted me to spend the next eight hours with her, in her bed, away from my son. The train doors opened at Pelham Parkway, Dinushka's station, and I knew I needed to give her an answer.

"Yes, I will," I said.

When I called Lauren to ask her if she could keep Jonathan overnight, I sensed her alarm. She opened with a kind of nervous laughter that I'd heard before, but she closed with, "I'll see you in the morning. Have fun and be careful!"

We were two blocks away from Dinushka's place when she suggested pizza from her favorite pizzeria. She handed me the keys to her apartment, explaining the trickiness of the lock and how to open the door. "Go, let yourself in, and I'll be there soon. Do you know how to get back to my building?"

"Yes," I said with weak confidence.

I tried repeatedly to unlock the apartment door. After many failed attempts, I was about to give up when Dinushka appeared carrying a pizza box and smiling widely. I handed her the keys, and she opened the door on the first try. We laughed for a bit about how long I'd been standing there when suddenly she leaned in and kissed me.

Our first kiss held up to my expectations and lasted longer than I would have thought. When we parted, we stepped over the threshold and into her apartment.

She would tell me later that while I was undressing in the privacy of her small bathroom, she knelt by her bed and prayed. While on bended knee, with her hand on her grandmother's tattered brown Bible, she spoke to God: "God, open my heart to your ways. Help me to love Nikkya for her heart, her soul, her body, her mind, without fear and anxiety. Allow me to love Nikkya and Jonathan in the way you want and the way they deserve. And let me receive the love I deserve, too. I feel your love around us. I ask for your blessings, Lord."

Dinushka had never had a one-night stand and wanted commitment in her life. As I pulled her oversized navy-blue T-shirt over my head, I wondered what this would turn into. I had no way of knowing, but I knew how I felt.

THE EARLY MORNING sun peeked through the curtains, casting a shadow across Dinushka's face. As I rolled over to look at her, the weight of my body woke her.

"Good morning," I said sheepishly.

"How'd you sleep?"

"I slept really well. I didn't wake up once to feed a baby."

I'd never spent a night away from Jonathan. I really wanted to stay wrapped in Dinushka's bed for the rest of the day, but I needed to get back to him. I readied myself, skipped taking a shower at her place, and got dressed. We walked side by side to my car. We kissed one last time, our fingers wrapped around each other's even after the kiss ended.

11

OVER THE NEXT few weeks, I traveled back and forth to New York to spend time with Dinushka on the weekends. We talked a lot about Jonathan, and I told her about his love of books and bath time, and how he loved hearing the sound of his own voice, even though the words only made sense to him. I told her that he loved Legos and the wooden block toys that I'd picked up for him at yard sales or welcomed as gifts from friends and family.

I wasn't ready to introduce Jonathan to Dinushka, still wary of her reaction but also afraid of shifting from "couple" to "couple and baby." She knew how much I worried about him when I was away, and though she never pushed too hard, she made it clear she'd be excited if I brought him with me when I visited her.

Reluctantly, I did. Jonathan was in my arms as we waited to be let in at the main entrance of Dinushka's apartment building. At eleven months old, his plump belly stretched out any onesie I'd put him in. At night, when I'd undress him, there'd be indents in his skin, in the inner part of his thigh, because he was getting too big for his clothes. My little baby was growing into a toddler. I kissed his chubby cheeks and inhaled that baby smell, which always helped me calm down some. When Dinushka opened her door, Jonathan slowly turned his head. As Dinushka walked toward us, she sensed his hesitation.

"Can I hold you, huh?" she asked, reaching out her arms to take him.

I held my breath, but within minutes they were laughing loudly together. She played and spoke with him as if they were reuniting, not meeting for the very first time. On Dinushka's face was the same smile I'd seen months ago on her profile photo— genuine and welcoming. Our dates morphed from sophisticated Manhattan restaurants and trips to art museums and independent movie theaters to playgrounds and parks, festivals and children's museums. On weekend nights, Jonathan slept peacefully in his Pack 'n Play while I slept in bed with Dinushka.

And just like that, two became three.

ON A HUMID afternoon I took Jonathan to the grocery store after work to buy baby food, WIC vouchers in hand. As I navigated the aisles, I listened to his full-bellied cackles resounding as I pretended the shopping cart was a helicopter. His baby teeth were coming in, and drool spilled out of his mouth. The moment I turned the shopping cart into the baby food aisle, my phone rang.

I answered with a "Well, hello there. How are you?" I couldn't help smiling.

"Hello!" Dinushka said in her booming voice. "What are you up to?"

"Oh, J and I are shopping for some baby food," I said. "Can you imagine eating this stuff?" I asked her, not really expecting a response.

"Yes. The applesauce is tasty. And it's a great way to lose weight," she joked.

"I'd like to start making his baby food. It will be so much better than this." I'd never tried to combine peas and milk in a blender, but making my kid's baby food seemed like something that moms with their own kitchens did. I immediately started fantasizing that maybe we would have a place of our own to call home one day.

"Nik, you're crazy. Make his baby food? That's so time-consuming."

"I know, but it's so much healthier."

"How's J doing?" Dinushka asked.

So far, she'd played with Jonathan in Central Park, introduced him to French fries and doughnuts, and bought him his very first Halloween costume—a tiny skunk outfit he wore to day care.

"He's fine. He's eyeing all the tiny jars. I hope he doesn't pull any of them down," I told her.

"I bet he's trying to grab at everything there," she said, and then her tone changed. "Nik, I called because I have a few minutes before I need to head to dinner at my parents' house."

"That sounds fun," I said, a tinge of longing in my voice.

I'd never thrown a nice dinner party for my mother, and now I never would.

"Oh yeah, loads," she said sarcastically. She told me she'd be bombarded by her Sri Lankan community asking when she would be getting married.

"Is everything okay?" I asked.

"Yes, everything is okay. I just . . . I want to say . . . I think . . ." She grew quiet.

"Say . . . what? You're kind of scaring me."

"I think I'm falling in love with you," she said.

"Well, that's good. Because I am falling in love with you, too."

That phone call lasted less than fifteen minutes, but it was a turning point for us. We'd only been dating for a month, but we could not deny our feelings.

Soon after, we made a decision: Jonathan and I would move into Dinushka's small studio apartment. We didn't make some big announcement, and it felt good to keep it just between us, without the pressure of explaining anything to anyone. And unlike so many of the other decisions in my life, this was one I made for myself and for my own happiness.

Next to Dinushka's futon bed, we set up Jonathan's playpen, the one that still doubled as his crib. Our clothes took up temporary space beside her dresser, packed in suitcases until we could figure out a more viable option. On our very first night all together, Jonathan slept between us, as if that's where he'd always been, right there, safely cuddled up with us. Ours.

I didn't sleep as well as Jonathan that first night. I heard every sound: Cars roaring down the one-way street in front of the apartment. Children crying. Spanish, English, and Jamaican-inflected English, all spoken in the span of fifteen minutes. New York City has always been a foreign place to me, and certainly not anywhere I had ever considered living. Nothing good ever happened there—or so I believed.

That was until I met Dinushka. She was the good thing and the reason I wanted to be there. Besides, Jonathan liked the city—he loved the Bronx Zoo, loved the food, the smells, the bustle. Dinushka, Jonathan, and I explored New York together. We moved through the boroughs, hoisting Jonathan's stroller up and down subway platforms. We bickered about what to give Jonathan for lunch.

We were both twenty-five, neither of us truly prepared to be a parent. I wondered how different we were from my own mother at that age. My mother had been running away from her child-hood traumas, and though she was no longer here, I was still coping with who my mother had become.

DINUSHKA AND I didn't get the opportunity to start off our rela-tionship alone together, like most couples. We didn't have the privilege of navigating our first argument without a baby staring up at us, didn't get the chance to sleep in on Saturday mornings or to roll out of bed and catch Sunday brunch.

One day, Dinushka reached a breaking point. I had left to pick up a few groceries and came back to Jonathan screaming. He had vomited all over the sheets, and Dinushka was covering her ears while trying to clean the bed.

"I can't do this," she said through gritted teeth.

I ended up talking her off the ledge, explaining why he might have thrown up, helping her wipe up while trying not to vomit myself.

Other issues developed. When Jonathan would reach for something that wasn't safe, Dinushka would yell loudly and grab him, her anxiety rising. I would worry about how angry she could get, her voice thundering. She had to lean into her nurturing and gentle side, as this did not come naturally to her. Maybe because she was a teacher, she often interacted with Jonathan in a didactic kind of way and had to learn that parenting was teaching but also more. When a kiss or an intimate moment was interrupted by a cry from Jonathan, I was nervous it would upset her. But this was part of parenthood, too, and I could only protect her so much from it. We were in it together.

What saved us was that she was never one to steer clear of challenging conversations. Each situation with Jonathan forced us to talk and reflect on our own childhoods—who we are as adults is so intricately tied to our upbringing.

"That's what families do, Nik. They talk things out." That was new for me. My family had kept a lot buried.

As for my relationship with Dinushka, my family tolerated it but didn't talk about it. As much as they loved me, I still wasn't sure they accepted me as a queer woman. I knew they didn't understand the challenges Dinushka and I faced as a couple, because in their eyes, we were just "two women." They didn't yet understand how two women could share a household like a man and a woman, or how two women could raise a child together.

I worried about what my grandparents would say when I told them I was in another serious relationship. I had called them in Virginia to let them know, prior to the move from Long Island to New York City, that I'd met someone new and that we'd been dating for a while. They didn't have much to say on the other end of the line. I imagined that after they hung up, they asked each other what the heck I was thinking, and said a prayer that eventually God would guide me in the right direction.

Despite our many roadblocks, all I could think was that I should follow my heart. And I did. No matter the challenges we faced, we were standing on a solid foundation, one we were building together, and it held all three of us.

THAT NOVEMBER, DINUSHKA and I had to make our first big family decision together. In order for me to fully move to New York City, to go to job interviews and get back to work, Jonathan would need childcare. Dinushka was with me every step of the way. We looked at a few day care centers in the city, but the prices were too high. I would qualify for state assistance, but first I needed a job.

We made the painfully difficult decision to send Jonathan to Virginia to stay with my grandparents until I found both a job and adequate childcare. I felt awful about it and didn't want to let him go, but there was just no safe, affordable option for him while we were both at work. As I folded his little clothes and packed his extra Pull-Ups, for some reason, the decision I'd made a while back to allow him to call me Mama really hit me. I realized there was something about *this* decision, about sending him to the safe home of my grandparents, that felt like a decision a mother would make. I knew that I loved him like a mother and that if we needed to be apart for a little while, so be it. I would do it for him.

A FEW WEEKS before Thanksgiving, I called Aunt She-She, the same aunt who would sit with me when I was a third and fourth grader, quizzing me as I'd prepare for social studies or math tests. I'd had anxiety as a student, freezing up and forgetting everything I'd studied so hard when it was time to take a test. But She-She was determined. She would quiz me over and over. She'd be stern and then frustrated, and our sessions often ended with tears streaming down my face. But she never gave up. "Nikki, you can do this," she would say. "Without the hard work, you won't get the results you're looking for."

Aunt She-She moved to Northern Virginia not long after Nanny and Poppy relocated there in the late 1990s. Now she agreed to meet me in halfway between New York and Virginia, to pick up Jonathan for his stay with my grandparents.

Dinushka joined us on the four-hour drive south to Delaware. Jonathan loved Dinushka's attention and kept reaching out his arms to her from the back seat. When she finally turned to him, a smile across her face, he would start babbling. She'd tell him stories, and although I wasn't convinced that he understood them, I appreciated how quiet they made him.

When we got to our drop-off point, we strapped Jonathan

into Aunt She-She's car, kissed and hugged him, and waved goodbye. Right away, Dinushka missed him so much that she wondered if we had made the wrong decision.

"Maybe we should have hired a babysitter for a few hours while you interview," she told me. "Then he could be with us every day."

Despite Dinushka's reservations, I knew I needed this time, and I trusted my grandparents. After all, I was a product of their child-rearing. I imagined She-She pulling into Nanny and Poppy's gravel driveway, honking her horn as her car approached the house. I imagined my grandparents meeting them on the front porch, Poppy's hands resting on his hips, my grandmother smiling so hard, because she couldn't contain her joy at having Jonathan with them.

I called every day, making sure Jonathan would remember my voice and who I was. "Your mama is on the phone," Nanny would say, and I could sense how uncomfortable she was using that word. Plus, I could tell my grandmother was getting increasingly attached to him.

"Nanny, I'm coming to get him soon. I know it'll be hard to let him go." I knew that Nanny had told herself the story that I, too, had believed for so long, that gay people could not have their own families. So not only was it disorienting for her to see me, her first grandchild, as a mother, but it was really tough for her to see that mother as a lesbian.

I made it down to visit Jonathan for Thanksgiving, and to celebrate his first birthday—a bit early but with all of the aunts and uncles who were visiting for the holiday. My shoes caught the gray gravel stones as I made my way to the square pavers, skipping like I did in elementary school across the playground, the anticipation building as I went up the three stairs leading to the front porch. Nanny opened the door, her orange nails, freshly manicured, glistening in the sun. I gave her a big hug, and held her a little tighter, my way of saying thank you for caring for Jonathan.

The house smelled wonderful, of yams doused with butter and brown sugar, and apple pie. Before I could even speak, Nanny let me know Jonathan was in the kitchen with Poppy. I walked in and gave Poppy a kiss on the cheek, then watched Jonathan running in circles around the room. His pace quickened when he saw my arms, open wide for a hug. A smile on his face, he made eye contact with me, but he didn't stop—instead, he kept running right past me. I reached out, grabbed his chubby, soft arm, and brought him close. Wearing his snug blue sleep n' play footies, he clapped his hands in excitement, his toes wiggling about.

For dinner, my grandparents sported their usual uniforms— Poppy in his gray sweatpants, Nanny in blue sweats, with a matching shirt. Her hair was dyed a honey blond and curled, ready for church. Poppy had a thin groomed mustache and a shiny bald head, and smelled clean, with a hint of cologne. I watched as my grandfather took the lid off the pot of neck bones and string beans and stuck a fork inside. My mouth watered. I was always hungry and particularly ready for the kind of home-cooked meal that I'd been missing.

I sat down at their Thanksgiving table to nicely browned

baked chicken, along with homemade macaroni and cheese, collard greens, string beans with smoked neck bones, and those yams. I thought about how many kids had passed through their kitchen before Jonathan. Their kids, the friends of their kids, the unexpected arrival of grandkids, the nieces and nephews who'd sought refuge from their own parents—all caught by their out-stretched arms, welcoming everyone into their home.

That first night at my grandparents', watching them move around their kitchen, I felt like the little girl they could still tell what to do, what to wear, or how much food I could put on my plate. The reality was, I was now a woman—a mother—and had something to prove to them. I needed my grandparents to understand that I wasn't throwing in the towel or giving up on raising this baby by letting him stay with them. It was true that he wasn't supposed to be mine, but now he was, and I was ready to fight for him.

My grandparents were so used to being the ones picking up the pieces after my mother's mistakes that I worried they saw Jonathan and me as just more pieces. And, sure enough, as I was cleaning the countertop and she was washing the last dish, Nanny said, "You might as well leave the boy here for us to raise." It felt like she'd waited until this exact moment to make the suggestion.

I knew then that I had to stand up to Nanny in a way that I had never done before. "I'm so grateful for your help, Nanny, and he will be here for a little while longer, but he's not staying forever," I said firmly.

DINUSHKA SPENT THAT Thanksgiving back in Connecticut. We didn't talk much over the holiday, both of us performing the roles our family expected to see from us during a festive time. We made the necessary small talk, smiled and pretended we weren't missing each other. When we could, we would sneak in a call, whispering into the phone, not letting our families know that our hearts were elsewhere.

In Virginia, after all the chicken, collard greens, and apple pie had been consumed, the hugs and kisses bestowed, the "Happy Birthday" song sung for Jonathan, and the birthday cards given, filled with what cash everyone could manage, I got into my car—without my son—and headed back home.

12

WE BOTH MISSED Jonathan, of course, but while he was in Virginia, Dinushka and I went on real dates. We drank a glass of wine with dinner, sometimes two. We stayed up late in bed, talking about our future together, sharing our career hopes and where we dreamed of living one day. This was what being a couple was supposed to be like at the very beginning—and we hadn't had much chance to experience being alone, just the two of us.

Dinushka was figuring out if she wanted to return to the classroom that following year, and she also had to decide when she would come out to her parents. Dinushka was an honest person, both with herself and with others. Unlike with Kate and me, it wasn't an issue of *if* Dinushka would come out; it was a matter of *when*. We both knew that it was an important and necessary step, especially if we were to be a family of three. Dinushka was growing more comfortable with her sexual identity, and in that regard, she was nothing like Kate, but I couldn't help but worry that keeping secrets from one's family was not healthy.

"What if my parents don't accept me and you, or Jonathan?" she said.

"Your parents will come around. Give them time. Once you come out, they will show you that they love you. You are their only daughter. Trust me."

All the stories she'd shared with me about her family made me feel optimistic. I hadn't met them yet, and only had her stories to go on, but I could sense the love they had for her.

I had my list of fears, too. What if I didn't find a job? What if we couldn't find a bigger apartment for the three of us?

Despite our concerns, life with Dinushka felt like magic. We were present for each other. We supported each other. I had someone who chose to love me for who I was, baby included. She had someone who saw her and who supported her dreams, even though I didn't necessarily understand how much she truly loved God. Both of us had been searching for this kind of love but didn't think we'd ever find it. Yet here we were.

Still, we were a gay couple planning our future with a little boy, and our worries about our legal rights to Jonathan never completely left us. On paper, I had only residential custody of Jonathan; Dinushka had no rights at all. We were raising Jonathan on the hope that Karl would not fight us—mostly because he'd never cared enough to ask for more.

DINUSHKA AND I spent our first Valentine's Day together like we did on the very first night we met. I planned to pick up dinner from the same pizza place—John & Joe's—and I thought I'd timed it perfectly. I'd run to get the food, have Dinushka's favorite wine open in the living room, and have Ben and Jerry's in the freezer for dessert. A simple, low-key celebration to mark five months together.

I realized while setting the table that I'd forgotten the ice cream. I dropped everything, ran out of the apartment, and raced to the store. I was out of breath by the time I got back. When I opened the door, Dinushka stood in front of me, tears streaming down her cheeks, her knitted brown cap slanted on the top of her head and about to fall to the ground.

"I thought you left me," she said, gripping the Valentine's Day card I'd written her. "You weren't here. I thought you wrote me this card as a goodbye and you were breaking up with me."

As I held her in my arms, I could feel her heart racing, her wet face against my cheek. I tried to make her feel safe, allowing the weight of my body to give her some comfort and reassurance, to let her know I was there.

"I would never break up with you in that way. But really, I'd never break up with you at all," I said, gently wiping the tears from her face. "I just ran out to get my two favorite men, Ben and Jerry. How can we celebrate without ice cream?"

She didn't laugh. I would discover, over time, much more about Dinushka's childhood and why she felt that I might reject her or hurt her in some way. Growing up, Dinushka was lonely; she experienced bullying and abuse that made her distrust others. It was her faith that enabled her to keep her fears at bay, or at least to not let them consume her. Hearing her, and the stories she shared with me about what she'd endured, touched me deeply. Her ability to be vulnerable with me allowed me to feel more and more comfortable being vulnerable with her. Sometimes we both let the tears fall, trusting that we'd have the other to wipe them away.

Dinushka and I had work to do in those months apart from Jonathan. We couldn't let the scars from our childhood or the newness of our relationship get in the way. We couldn't waste one day mulling over small issues, like who didn't put the toothpaste cap back on, or wallowing in the hurt of one of us checking out someone else. Our mission was to bring Jonathan back from my grandparents as quickly as possible.

Luckily, I'd found a new job, in Midtown Manhattan. I'd be an administrative assistant to the vice president of the nonprofit Junior Achievement, helping K–12 kids learn something I'd never learned myself: how to handle money. I'd have to travel from the Bronx into Manhattan by myself, which was daunting, but I was making progress toward reuniting with Jonathan.

When I'd call Jonathan, before putting him on the phone to hear my voice, my grandmother would say, "You know, you can let him stay here. We can get him started in school." Her words would trail off as she waited for my response. It was like she refused to listen to me, like I had not made it clear that Jonathan's stay there was to be only for a short time. Her lack of acknowledgment cut me, reminding me of the feeling I had when she'd swatted me with a switch as a child.

"No, I'll get him soon. This is temporary," I repeated each time. "But thank you both for being here for me, for us." I didn't remind her that when Jonathan was born, she was sure she was too old to raise another child.

After my three-month review at Junior Achievement, I received an offer to join the JA team as a permanent staff member, and finally it felt like I could really plan for Jonathan's return. I was determined to piece together a life for him that would provide him with all the things I wanted for myself: safety, stability, and family.

DINUSHKA AND I knew that what we were experiencing together—dates on Arthur Avenue for authentic Italian, hours spent on Saturday afternoons at our favorite coffee spot in Greenwich Village—would not be ours forever. We were never and would never be a "new couple"—we had old-couple problems, and old-couple decisions to make.

With Jonathan and now Dinushka in my life, things began to make sense. When I fumbled at work, I knew I could come home at five and fall into Dinushka's arms. My paychecks were small, but I was a program assistant—I'd never had a title that sounded so impressive—and the money meant I was contributing to household costs.

On the nights when Dinushka brought work home, she would sit at her small white desk, her wicker chair creaking with every swipe of her red pen across her students' papers. I felt such peace watching her. I would lie on the futon, journaling, pausing between sentences to take in this warm and happy scene. At bedtime, when we put our heads down on our pillows, the glow of a streetlight illuminated both of our faces.

"So what are you going to do?" I asked Dinushka. I knew she didn't want to keep teaching, but she still hadn't yet made the decision to leave.

"I want to serve God," she said. "Sometimes I truly feel more like a minister, talking to these kids about their personal issues, their families, and even their spirituality. I want to give the sacrament. I want to follow whatever call he has for me."

The ease in which she described her relationship with God moved me. I identified as spiritual and believed in the power of prayer and ritual, but I'd never felt like the Baptist Church, which I'd grown up in, was the place for me. We were so honest with each other about most things, but I couldn't bring myself to tell Dinushka that I was unsure of what my relationship was with God.

Sitting in the pew on Sundays as a child, eyes closing as the sermon rounded the forty-five-minute mark, was the lens through which I viewed religion. The roles I saw women in were that of support staff—ushers or choir directors. The wives of the preachers followed a particular code, dressing in fashionable suits with coordinating hats. I could not relate, and I certainly couldn't see myself as a minister's wife.

From time to time, Nanny would share with me the story of my wanting to be baptized at five years old.

"You walked right up to the pastor at First Baptist Church and said, straight-faced, without blinking, 'I want to be baptized.' And that was it. You were so young he wasn't sure you knew what you were saying exactly, and neither were we. But you kept asking, so not long after, we dressed you in your white robe. Our miracle baby."

Even though there'd been so many times I'd question my life—why my father could never be a dad to me, why I still carried so much anger toward my mother, why I had to fight so hard for custody of Jonathan, and even why my skin was so dark or my hair was so kinky—but I still prayed and kept faith in my own way. While living with Dinushka, my own relationship with God slowly began to change in subtle ways. In our conversations about religion, I realized that I was angry at him. Maybe I needed to forgive him for letting me down.

I had a calling, too; my desire to have more kids was as powerful as Dinushka's faith.

"You said you want two or three more kids?" she asked one night, our bodies squeezed tightly together in bed.

Dinushka was uncertain about more children. One was enough for her. I told her again, with conviction, that I wanted to be pregnant and carry a baby, and was unwilling to compromise. At first, I couldn't imagine it. But living in New York, I saw more queer families, and that helped me see that it was possible.

"Probably two. Maybe three. I want the chance to have a baby."

"But you have Jonathan," she said.

"Yes, and I want to give him siblings. I want all of us to live in the same house. I want to add to this story."

Dinushka went silent for a moment, and then she talked about her own struggles with identity, being queer, and creating a family that we'd been told was not "natural." Dinushka had never dreamed of being married or even owning a home. Long ago, she'd come to the conclusion that her queerness would put limits on her life, which was something I understood. I had once felt I couldn't have what other people had.

But now I wanted it all: the house, the kids, the married

life. And maybe Dinushka was opting out of all that not only because she queer; maybe we just wanted different things. She found meaning in church, and on long walks pondering God, and in giving her last five dollars to a homeless person. She saw her purpose as the opportunity to serve God, and I saw mine as the opportunity to be loved and to love others wholly.

When Jonathan finally returned to us that April, after almost six months in Virginia, Dinushka began to question all that she thought she wanted.

PART THREE

13

———

DRIVING THE LONG stretch of the New Jersey Turnpike, then passing through Pennsylvania, Delaware, and Maryland, it felt just like our college days on the way to Virginia Beach for spring break. Dinushka couldn't get away, and Lauren had accepted my invitation to accompany me on the eight-hour trip to Northern Virginia to pick up Jonathan, who was waiting at my aunt She-She's house. Every so often, I'd glance over at her and watch her push up her glasses, which kept falling down her nose. She didn't have the obligations I did, and I wondered what she thought of all this.

I was lucky that Lauren was always there for me, especially during this time when my life was such a mess. She was a good friend. I had been so grateful she watched Jonathan during my first date with Dinushka, and now, here she was again, by my side supporting me in this new chapter of motherhood.

The moment we pulled into my aunt's driveway, panic set in. I hadn't seen Jonathan since Christmas, and now it was April.

Would he remember me? What if he didn't? My hands were sweaty, and my chest was tight. I tried to pretend I was simply excited to be seeing Jonathan, but really I was feeling worried and afraid. Before I went inside, I said a little prayer to myself. *Lord, please allow my bond with Jonathan to be felt by us both.*

When Lauren and I entered the house, gave the obligatory hugs—much of my family had assembled at She-She's—and looked around the living room, I didn't see Jonathan.

"Where is he?" I asked, my voice shaking.

My aunt had taken him out to the yard, so I walked back out of the house and made my way to the play area. I took a long look at the slide to see if it was, in fact, Jonathan gliding down like a big boy.

He was walking and running—both firsts I'd missed with him.

Even with my daily calls, I had lost so much. I stood frozen as he waddled away from the bottom of the slide, both feet solidly on the ground. He was wrapped snug in a blue fleece hat that closed under his chin with Velcro, a blue-and-white striped shirt, and jean overalls. I could hear his deep belly laugh, and, with that, I couldn't stop smiling. I looked over at Lauren and saw that she was smiling just as wide as I was.

I watched as Jonathan climbed up to the top of the slide to do it all over again. He was committed to doing things on his own, swatting my aunt away. He had his back to me as I began to walk toward him. When Jonathan turned around and spotted me, he froze, seeming stunned. In the short amount of time it took me to reach him, a regretfulness set in, and I vowed never to leave him that long again. I called out to him as I got closer—once, twice, three times—until finally he began to move toward my voice. Then he started running to me. *My son knows me*, I thought.

What I'd feared most hadn't happened.

I held him as tight as I could and swung him around. I put my nose in the crease of his neck to remind myself of his smell, but this time he smelled different. He wasn't a baby anymore. His softness had changed to something I couldn't quite put my finger on.

I admit I held him too long in those first few moments. Even as he squirmed to free himself, I held on. Seeing his sweet face again made me remember why I'd taken on this responsibility.

He needed a mother. He needed me.

I ONLY STAYED one night at my aunt's house, but it was long enough to hear lots of stories from Jonathan's stay in Virginia. I sat on the tan leather couch, taking it all in, while Lauren sat in the middle of the floor, playing peekaboo with Jonathan. My aunts, uncles, and grandparents were all good storytellers. It was like being in an episode of *Good Times* (with my aunts and uncles) or *The Jeffersons* (with my grandparents.)

"One day, I was playing outside with him and I told him not to leave my side, and when I turned around he was gone," my grandfather began. "He took off, booking it down to the neighbor's house. I knew they had a pool, so I ran after him." Poppy stood up, his navy-blue sweatpants suit fitting snug around his waist, and he playfully raced to the other side of the room so we all would truly understand how fast Jonathan took off. He told the story with a mix of joy and sternness I remembered from my own childhood, like the time he scolded me for breaking a window in our house but forgave me moments later because "we all make mistakes." With both me and Jonathan, he set a tone—one that said I love you and forgive you all in one breath.

Jonathan never made it to the neighbor's house, of course. My grandfather, out of breath and sweating, caught up to him. A reactionary swat on Jonathan's hand gave my grandfather the false sense of security that Jonathan would not run away again. Again, I remembered my own childhood and the times I had defied my grandparents—sneaking out of the house when I was supposed to be in a time-out, sitting on the riding lawn mower when I was told not to. But now, I could feel the sting of that slap on Jonathan's hand much harder than anything I had endured.

"Slapping him won't stop him," I said quietly.

Poppy didn't respond.

"He's a good eater, Nikki," my grandmother chimed in, changing the subject. "He ate all of my good cookin'."

My grandparents' stories made me realize that Jonathan got to make memories with them. They needed him, too—to remind them of my mother, to remind them that she'd birthed him into this world—and he was a living, breathing reminder of the hope they'd had for her as a child. By having him in their home, I think they also came to see that I was doing the right thing, and that I was doing a good job.

Suddenly, the worry and fear I'd carried during those months Jonathan was with my grandparents lifted as I watched him walk around their living room confidently. He looked so independent, so sure of himself. The choice Dinushka and I had made to send him away was nothing like what my mother had done to me. He was *my* baby, and now I was bringing him home.

The next morning, Lauren and I loaded up the car to begin our journey back to New York. I was afraid Jonathan would cry for Nanny and Poppy, but he hugged them goodbye and hopped into the car with an ease that eased *me*.

WHEN WE GOT back to the Bronx, Dinushka came out to help us unpack the car. She bypassed me—no hug or kiss—and went right to Jonathan. But when she offered her hand to him, he only stared back at her. There was no waving to get her attention. No laughing. No expression of excitement. Nothing at all. Still, she picked him up out of his car seat and held him to her chest.

When we got to the apartment, Dinushka excitedly showed Jonathan all the new things she got him—a stuffed Elmo toy, a new Elmo bed, and an Elmo plush chair for him to sit in—and he began to relax and play. He was only a baby when he'd left us. We both had to accept that we all would need time to rebuild what we'd had.

In bed later that night, as Jonathan slept a few feet away from us, Dinushka and I talked.

"My heart was broken when he didn't recognize me, Nik," she said. "He didn't even try to show me affection. He sees me as a stranger."

After a few days, Dinushka's studio apartment felt claustrophobic; we were all on top of one another. Dinushka and I began bickering. Things that once didn't matter started to matter so much more—like whether or not I had money in my savings account and how I disciplined Jonathan. With him now in the toddler stage, he would pull things down, anytime and anywhere. He'd scream for no reason we could figure out. And at some point, he'd learned the word *no*. His baby stage, the time when he'd stay put and when his adorable babble brought such comfort to me, had disappeared.

We found a home day care in the apartment of a sweet, older Spanish-speaking woman and were hopeful that Jonathan would learn from some of the other kids in her care. She was affordable—about a hundred dollars a week—though even that was a stretch for us. But after his first full day there, we couldn't find him at pickup time. I felt scared. There was a language barrier, and the handful of words I knew in Spanish didn't help me to locate my son. As we walked around her apartment, looking into all the children's faces, I knew this wasn't going to work. We eventually found him under the kitchen table, alone.

I wasn't the best with money. I'd always paid my bills on time, but I hadn't been taught how to think long-term, hadn't learned about the value of putting something aside from each paycheck, saving for retirement, or investing in mutual funds. I'd always thought I could parent alone, but now that Jonathan was getting older it became more apparent that I was having a hard time providing for him without depending on Dinushka. The fear that I was draining her financially—and that Jonathan was draining her emotionally—scared me. I needed us all to be okay.

I decided it was important to give Dinushka some space, so even though it was financial strain, I signed a lease on an apartment three floors up from her studio, a one-bedroom with a large living room and a galley-style kitchen whose tan floor tiles showed their age. Dinushka helped me with the security deposit, and my uncle Bob helped me with the first month's rent.

Some nights, we would eat dinner in her fully furnished apartment instead of in my empty one. But every night, Dinushka and I would go back to our respective apartments. It felt silly to live separately, but it also felt necessary. I was constantly struggling—struggling to find a job, struggling to pay my bills, struggling to furnish my apartment. I didn't want to make her struggle along with me.

One night, I asked if she'd give me a break and bathe Jonathan in her apartment while I took thirty minutes to myself. She reluctantly agreed. She kept some of his clothes in her apartment, and she had all she needed to give him his nighttime bath. Still, I could almost see the fear in her eyes—fear that something would go wrong.

Fifteen minutes later, I heard a knock on my door.

"Who is it?"

"It's me. Can you let me in?"

As soon as I opened the door, Dinushka rushed past me, putting Jonathan down on the floor.

"Did something happen?"

"He vomited all over my bed as soon as you left. I put him in the tub, and he was crying and crying and crying. I don't know why. He refused to let me bathe him, and just kept shouting 'No' at me."

I could feel her frustration.

"Nik, I can't do this," she continued. "I can't be a parent. This is not for me."

"I'll help you clean up. It's not easy doing all of this. But you can do it."

"I just can't. I can't commit to this, to you, to him. I'm sorry," she said.

I took a deep breath. Silence filled the space where my words should have been. I had nothing to say.

As the door closed behind her, I tasted my tears. I sat on the wooden floor in my empty apartment, desperately wishing I could redo the entire last hour. *Maybe if I hadn't needed a break... Maybe if I had stayed longer at her place... Maybe if I'd given Jonathan a bath myself...* I wasn't ready for it to be over between us.

That night, as I replayed our conversation over and over in my head, I knew I still had a fight in me to keep Dinushka in my life. I sat down and wrote her a letter, putting down on paper everything I felt.

I knew this would not be easy. You knew it, too. You need to know that I love you. I do. If you need to leave, I understand—this life is challenging and complicated even more by the unknowns ahead. I never wanted you to change anything about yourself. Please know that you have a piece of my heart and I love you.

For the first time in my life, I didn't want to use a backup plan. I wanted to throw away plan B.

I picked up Jonathan, hoisted him onto my right hip, grabbed my keys, and headed downstairs to Dinushka's apartment. During the quick elevator ride to the first floor, I felt guilty for getting her involved in my turbulent life, but as I bent down to stuff my handwritten note underneath her door, I reminded myself that she was a grown woman. I'd been honest with her from our very beginning; she knew who I was and the responsibilities I had assumed.

As the elevator doors again closed in front of us, I went to my go-to prayer, a short and sweet request: *Dear God, if this is meant to be, please let it be. Amen.*

Almost as soon as I got back upstairs and put Jonathan on the air mattress, my phone rang.

"I got your note," Dinushka said. "I love you, too. I don't want to lose what we have together. I am scared and nervous, and it's a change in my life. It's different from what I thought it would be." Dinushka told me she found it difficult to adjust to what a relationship looked like for us. It meant Jonathan, it meant me, it meant sharing an apartment, and it meant being messy. She told me she knew she had more to learn about love, but that she was starting to understand it by loving Jonathan and me. This life that she'd never envisioned for herself, ever, was just plain hard for her, she said, but she also told me that she didn't want to let me go.

I had imagined so many scenes of my life with Jonathan: Sunday morning breakfast, playing in our backyard, walking him to his school bus, making him a home-cooked dinner. But now I kept seeing Dinushka with us in those scenes: coming home in the afternoon to sit around our long wooden dining room table, the babies we'd have together, and the dogs running through *our* backyard.

Maybe those dreams could be real.

THAT AUGUST, THREE months before Dinushka's twenty-seventh birthday, she moved into the one-bedroom apartment upstairs. Dinushka asked a few of her friends for help furnishing it—we'd hauled up everything from her studio apartment but this place was so much larger—and they came through. The apartment would soon fill up with everything we needed by way of good-hearted people who loved Dinushka and barely knew I existed.

I cannot remember how or why we decided to do this, but one evening we rented a U-Haul and Dinushka drove us from the Bronx and into Manhattan to pick up everything. She is not the best driver, and I held the door panel the entire way, praying that we would get back to the apartment safely. In the dark, we loaded the U-Haul and then we made our way back home. With small tables, a hand-me-down bed, a sofa, and even dishes and silverware, our apartment soon became our refuge, the place we could live and be together without outside static.

ON OUR FIRST Christmas Eve together in our new home, after a homemade dinner of Cornish hen, string beans, and mashed potatoes, Dinushka decided she had to find a way to tell her family about us. It was Jonathan who helped her realize what this commitment really meant. The week before, Dinushka's father had visited her at the apartment, which he had no idea we shared. He met her just outside our building to drop off a home-cooked meal made by her mother: chicken curry and rice. Carrying the white plastic bag full of food, he approached the front door, where Dinushka stood with Jonathan in his blue stroller. As Jonathan's chubby brown hand struggled to pull out a handful of Honey Nut Cheerios, he looked up and into the face of Dinushka's father, whose voice boomed a "Hellooo . . ." over the din of the Bronx streets. Dinushka's father bent down, unaware of who the child was, and Jonathan offered him a smile and a soggy Cheerio. He couldn't help but smile back at Jonathan. Dinushka decided that she could not go on denying who we were or what we were to her—not to strangers or to her parents. Jonathan needed his parents to stand up for him.

That Christmas Eve, we put Jonathan to bed, then set out his gifts from Santa on the sofa and around the tiny Christmas tree. We snuggled together and talked about how the very next day Dinushka would leave to spend Christmas Day with her parents in Connecticut and come out to them, and I would travel to Long Island to visit my family. A few weeks before, Karl had reentered our lives, calling me out of the blue, shouting that he hadn't seen his son and demanding a meeting. I'd put off the visit until after Christmas, but Dinushka was plunging into her own uncomfortable visit now.

In the end, Dinushka didn't find the courage to tell her whole extended family about us. Celebrating Christmas over drinks with her parents and aunts and uncles, she nodded her head when they asked her if she was single. She became emotional when she told me that she had failed, that she had gone into the guest bathroom to cry alone. She'd felt such shame denying my existence, denying Jonathan's.

But after the party ended, and away from the rest of her family and friends, Dinushka took her parents into their living room. She had already come out to her brother a little bit earlier but had sworn him to secrecy. In the room where their Christmas tree sat each year, where she'd grown up playing board games and the piano, she finally shared with her parents that she was in love and living with a woman. It all came out, in one conversation, amidst tears and raised voices. Her mother stood, finger pointed at Dinushka, and her father crossed his arms in anger.

Dinushka's brother knew she'd wanted to tell their parents at Christmas and supported her decision to do so. He'd wanted her to wait for him so that he could be by her side, as he was traveling back from his wife's family's Christmas. But she felt it was something she needed to do on her own.

Soon after the tears began to fall, and emotions were high, her brother finally arrived, walked in, and intervened, reminding their parents of how much they loved their daughter, warning them that pushing her away, not accepting her for who she was, meant they didn't love her, and they all knew that they did love her. They were all family, no matter what.

She returned to me, to our apartment, drained and exhausted. Her parents told her that they couldn't see or talk to her.

Eventually, though, they did call. The phone conversations were long, with more of their tears and yelling. Dinushka remained calm, praying after every call that they'd know and feel her love for me. She would tell me that she prayed they'd remember who she was, someone who followed her heart and spoke to God in every situation.

WITH OUR APARTMENT settled, we focused on finding a new day care. Jonathan had been attending one for a little over a month before it rubbed me the wrong way, with too many kids and not enough stimulation. My maternal instinct told me it was again time to move him, and this time the right place came along—it took state subsidies, and the space was clean and well maintained.

Finding childcare also required us to figure out how to describe Dinushka's role to strangers and ultimately to ourselves. She wasn't comfortable being called Mom or Mama but wanted something that easily fit both her and Jonathan. Dinushka was hard to pronounce for some people and especially for a toddler, so she decided that Jonathan would call her Di-Di.

What we didn't anticipate is that one day of his own accord he would call her Da Da, and that our queer family would take shape right in front of us.

IN THE MIDST of all these changes, I had received that call from Karl. Dinushka stood just steps away as he asked about Jonathan and then had me put him on the phone.

Once I had the phone back, Karl started in on me. "You never bring him to see me, like something is wrong with me and my family."

I was hot, scared, and unsure. I took a breath and readied myself to speak, but he continued.

"If you don't start bringing him to see me, then you leave me with no other choice. We are just gonna have to go to court."

I was angry now.

"You can call any time and come and see him," I said. "All you need to do is tell me when, and we can make it work."

I wondered if he sensed the fear and worry in my voice.

"Well, maybe you should just take Jonathan out to see him," Dinushka said after we ended the call. "He'll get bored after a few visits." She sounded more confident than I felt, but I called Karl and set up a visit at the aquarium where he worked.

Dinushka, Jonathan, and I arrived exactly on time, my hand shaky as I unbuckled Jonathan from his car seat. I placed him on the ground, grabbed his hand, and together the three of us began to walk toward the entrance.

"How are you feeling?" Dinushka asked before we went inside.

"I am ready for this to be over and it hasn't even started yet."

I thought about how Dinushka had chosen to live with us after dealing with Karl. This was not a normal life for anyone, but especially not compared to Dinushka's family.

What looked like a college student was at the aquarium front desk, I assumed at her weekend job, and we told her who we were there to see. Karl worked maintenance, cleaning up after guests in the cafeteria, unclogging toilets, and ensuring that the buildings and grounds were kept up. She radioed him with her black walkie-talkie, and we waited.

"Hey, J," he called from a distance when he saw us. "It's Daddy!"

Jonathan stood next to my leg, unsure what to do, then looked up at Dinushka—his Di-Di—for some reassurance. At one and a half years old, he hadn't ever spent a full day with his "daddy." In fact he hadn't seen Karl much at all in the last year; the few times Karl had called, I'd told him that Jonathan was in Virginia, and I could hear his aggravation building, because I hadn't asked him for permission to send him there. I knew my mother would not have asked him for permission either. I also knew that Karl was afraid to call my grandparents' home, scared of what they'd say to him, worried they'd be angry for getting my mother pregnant and then not being there for her.

I tapped Jonathan on his shoulder. "Do you want me to go with you to say hi?"

He nodded yes.

I held Jonathan's chubby little hand, and we walked side by side toward Karl. When he bent down to hug Jonathan, I could smell the sweat staining his green shirt.

"Do you wanna go see some animals?" he asked.

Jonathan's response came by way of a nod.

I glanced back at Dinushka and waved her over. Karl looked her up and down, like he was unsure of what to make of her short haircut, her glasses, the smile on her face whenever she looked at Jonathan.

Karl wanted to eat something first, so the four of us went to the cafeteria to grab lunch, where Dinushka and I spent ten minutes trying to convince Jonathan to try something other than his usual macaroni and cheese, apples, and French fries. He finally opted for a hot dog, and then we all sat down at a tiny square table and made uncomfortable small talk.

I knew that Karl loved to talk about himself, so we let him. We asked him question after question: How long have you worked here? Do you work weekends? Do they pay well? Do you like your job?

An hour later, he told us that he needed to get back to work but that we were free to walk around for as long as we wanted. I'd already known he would leave us to do the heavy lifting of showing Jonathan around. I wondered how he would react if we told him we didn't actually want to be there at all.

We got up, cleaned off our table, and walked outside to see the penguins and sea lions. My nerves began to calm when I was alone with Dinushka and Jonathan.

"Well, that was awkward," I said softly and with a smile, just in case Karl was around the corner.

When it was time to go, Karl met us at the entrance to say goodbye. Sweat was beading on his forehead. "Did you guys have fun?" he asked.

"Yeah, we had a good time," I said. "Didn't we, J?"

Jonathan nodded. Karl waved us goodbye, gave Jonathan a high five, and told us to get home safe.

On the two-hour car ride home, Dinushka and I were too

tired to talk. We were emotionally exhausted from having to put on a show, lying about how we were truly feeling.

There would be more visits, Karl barely present at any of them, always distracted by something—the job, his phone, other people. We thought about the sacrifices we were making, the things we were giving up so that Karl could say he'd had a visit with Jonathan. Karl also seemed to view Dinushka with a kind of disdain or suspicion, and after a few meetings and the same looks I realized he was threatened by her.

Then I received a certified letter summoning me to court—a petition from Karl for full custody. He wanted to take Jonathan from me—from us—and erase all that we'd created together.

14

IT WAS AS if we were going into battle. We needed armor, and for that I called on everyone we knew. I reached out to friends from high school, including one who also happened to be a Child Protective Services caseworker in the very county in which we'd be going to court. She knew me as the girl in high school who was never late to class, who would always help a classmate in need, who would never give up. She wrote a character letter:

> Despite Nikkya's arduous path early on, she always continued to maintain a positive outlook on life and shared her enthusiasm with others. Nikkya independently supported herself through her college years, and although she was close to achieving what she had desired academically and professionally (becoming a doctor), she left everything behind and chose a life that revolved around raising her brother.

A mentor who supervised me when I volunteered as a crisis counselor wrote a letter. My current boss at the nonprofit wrote a letter about my work ethic, using words like honesty, reliability, and integrity. Another letter from a friend read: "When Nikkya filed for custody of her brother, it was the most unselfish choice I have ever witnessed a person make. But for Nikkya it was never a choice but instead a role she knew was meant for her to fulfill."

Then there were the words from my supervisor at Junior Achievement of New York: "Nikkya is exceedingly self-aware and self-understanding. She impresses her coworkers as level-headed, tremendously poised, and mature. Many times, I have turned to Nikkya for advice and as a sounding board."

In addition, Dinushka reached out to a former colleague whose father was an antitrust lawyer, asking if he could help us find someone to represent us pro bono. Within a matter of days, we were connected with Mr. Hill, a family lawyer willing to take our case. He was white, with thinning gray hair and red-flushed cheeks. On the phone, his tone was soft and quiet, as if he needed to deliver a message in secret.

"Well, you know, Nikkya, this isn't going to be easy. You are not the biological parent. But you do have a chance, given your relationship to the child."

I knew Dinushka was torn on the topic of custody—we both were. What was the right choice for Jonathan? Should I push for sole custody with no visitation rights for Karl? Accept some sort of joint custody? We thought that Jonathan would eventually want to know what his story was, and Dinushka and I considered that perhaps that story should be told by Karl. "Maybe it's good for him to know his father," Dinushka said before our meeting with Mr. Hill. "Then he can decide for himself when he's older if he wants a deeper relationship." We wanted to think clearly about what Jonathan might want in the future.

Early one Monday morning, Dinushka and I drove to Long Island to meet Mr. Hill at his office in a historic house on the same road that took us to Karl's aquarium. The interior felt cold, reflecting the transactional nature of custody disputes.

Mom gives up this, Dad receives that.

Though, of course, isn't it always emotional? We were both wrecks as we sat down in Mr. Hill's dark-green office chairs, gripping the armrests for dear life. I focused on his round belly kissing the front of a desk overflowing with stacks of papers. Mr. Hill told us this: I did not have a very good chance of winning custody of Jonathan. He spoke in a matter-of-fact way, making me feel like he didn't really care about what happened to Jonathan or us. He was working for free, and I couldn't help feeling that in his eyes I was just another Black single mother, fulfilling the stereotype. He asked no questions and seemed to have no interest in who I really was. And because Dinushka had no role, shared no blood with Jonathan, he didn't ask her any questions either.

"Karl is the biological father," he said. A powerful sentence telling me who the law favored, no matter how much or how little that person cared for their child.

I stared blankly at my new lawyer, trapped somewhere between despair and anger. Karl's reputation on the streets was that he jumped from woman to woman—lying, cheating, and drinking his way through relationships. When he was not occupied by a woman, he tried his hand at selling drugs. He always found trouble.

Then I looked at Dinushka holding back her tears, and I yearned for her to say something to comfort me. I silently searched her face, knowing she would tell me that God will give Jonathan the family he needs—even if that family is not us. Dinushka's family was close, and she had a strong bond with her own father. I thought this clouded her judgment and made her unable to understand what a dysfunctional family or a deadbeat dad looked like. I was the expert here. As mad and confused as Dinushka's dad had been when she'd come out, he had never withheld his love.

Dinushka didn't understand how vindictive Karl could be. He was the one who'd wanted a paternity test, stalling and avoiding taking responsibility for Jonathan. He was the one who'd wanted us to bring Jonathan to him, never wanting to meet us halfway. I was sure this would be no different, that he was doing this just to assert his power over me.

Later, Dinushka would tell me that she was only trying to be hopeful, even though inside she felt a constant stabbing in her heart, a fear that life would never be the same, that we would lose Jonathan. She had noticed, of course, the lack of care, attention, and affection Karl showed toward Jonathan, how he called so rarely, never sent a card, never attempted to visit.

"You are only his half sister," Mr. Hill told me again, as if I had forgotten my place. "We have two choices. We can ask for sole custody, but then you run the risk of losing him completely. Or you could come to some sort of agreement with his father before ever getting in front of the judge."

"Isn't the whole point of this to go in front of the judge and let him decide?"

"You could, if it gets to that," Mr. Hill continued. "Or you and Karl can talk and agree to terms that we can make into a legal agreement. If you can agree outside of the chambers, you have a better shot at keeping Jonathan."

Negotiate for my son? It didn't make sense to me, but after our conversation with the lawyer, I decided to try to come to terms with Karl without a judge.

EVEN THOUGH WE would not be negotiating in court, the meeting took place at the family court building. When we arrived, Nanny, Lady, and Aunt She-She were waiting for us in the parking lot. The baby of Nanny's six kids, Aunt She-She spoke with a competence, a finesse I longed to have: a smooth, straightforward delivery, no matter the situation. Lady's passionate indignation was the complete opposite. I needed both of them at that moment. Maybe their words would knock some sense into Karl.

I could tell Dinushka was nervous by the way she stood, not saying much, her hands tucked into the pockets of her soft velvet green blazer. I quickly introduced her to my family, not knowing if she was more jittery about meeting them, or meeting them *here*, or going to family court. They greeted her politely, but all of us felt strained under the pressure.

Together we walked through the automatic doors and stood

in line to be searched by two guards, one a white woman and the other a Black man, both reminding me of all the times I went to visit my mother in jail. I felt as if I was again somehow being punished for my mother's sins.

With each step forward in the line, it became difficult for me to hide my emotions. The first check was completed, then the next, a handheld wand scanning my body. Surely the guards could see the sweat gathering on my top lip and the pained look on my face, hear the shakiness in my voice as I answered their questions.

I walked toward an uncertain future, joining the other broken families in the waiting area. There were Black men and women sitting seats apart, lines of stress etched into their foreheads, anger hot in their voices as they told their kids to sit down. I heard some families speaking Spanish, their skin tanned from the sun, and imagined they were from the farms on eastern Long Island, day laborers working hard to keep food on the table for their families.

When we were finally called into the interrogation room, it was like something you'd see in a *Law & Order* episode. Karl sat next to his lawyer on one side of a long wooden table, with Mr. Hill and me on the other. Karl looked thinner than I remembered him. His skin was also two shades darker, like burned toast. He was clean-shaven, dressed in black jeans, a T-shirt, and white sneakers, trying hard to project some sort of swagger but falling short.

"Why do you think Jonathan should stay in your care?" his lawyer asked me.

I needed to be dispassionate and articulate without sounding judgmental. I needed to show that I understood why Jonathan's father wanted a relationship with him and the importance of that, even though I knew his intentions weren't honest and believed his desire for Jonathan was about controlling me.

"Jonathan deserves to stay in my home because I've had him from day one," I said.

"Why is your home better than where he is?" Mr. Hill asked Karl.

"I am his father," Karl said, barely audible.

"Don't you think a child is meant to be with its biological parent?" his lawyer asked me.

"I was raised by my grandparents. They were not my biological parents. I turned out okay."

"Why would you want to rip him from where he is currently to have him live with you?" Mr. Hill asked Karl.

"He is my son, and I want to have a relationship with him," Karl said. "He deserves that."

I tried to listen to Karl's reasoning. His words flowed as if he'd practiced them the night before. I saw his bloodshot eyes but didn't linger long enough to stare. I wondered if he'd stayed up late drinking.

Dinushka and my family anxiously sat outside the small room that Karl and I were holed up in. During breaks, I updated them about what had happened behind the closed doors.

THERE WERE WEEKS of discussions. Every time I entered that small room with Karl and our two white lawyers, I was furious.

The lawyers sat in their dark suits and buttoned-up collared shirts with ties hanging down, their hands folded atop the brown folders that held the story of Jonathan's life inside. I knew I was not my mother, but I felt I was being treated as if I were. And when I shared what my mother would have wanted for Jonathan, I felt ignored. They said, "Ms. Hargrove, we understand your frustration with this process." But their words felt condescending and patronizing, and their demeanor told me I would lose this fight.

15

IT WAS LIKE buying a car—a little haggling for a lower price or a longer warranty, hoping to make a deal. My lawyer had urged me to offer as much to Jonathan's biological father as I could muster, an effort that would help ensure that I wouldn't lose custody. After meeting almost monthly in what felt like the principal's office, Karl and I finally came to a mediated agreement on December 3, 2008. I would keep residential custody, and starting in January, Karl would have Jonathan two weekends a month, one week every summer, and a visit on his birthday every November. We'd alternate holidays—Christmas, Thanksgiving, and Easter—while Karl would get every Father's Day. I agreed to drive Jonathan to and from each visit.

For months, I had sat in a room with three men, none of whom I really knew. They all professed to have Jonathan's best interests at heart. I felt relieved that Jonathan would remain with Dinushka and me but sick that I didn't actually win this battle. Karl was ordered to pay child support—$123 every two weeks—retroactively from the month I was given custody. It was a small sum that would only cover the cost of gas and tolls to drive Jonathan to and from Long Island. I knew he would miss many payments in the months to come, but Dinushka reminded me that God, and our commitment to Jonathan, would continue to provide for us, even without Karl's support.

Mr. Hill seemed pleased to no longer have to work for free. If we needed to, we could request a visitation modification, but that would mean returning to court and letting the judge render a decision. I never intended to go back—I didn't want to put my family in a situation that could lead to us losing Jonathan forever. We agreed we would only return to court if Jonathan was at risk. We prayed that he would be safe during the visits with Karl.

For Jonathan's first overnight visit, Dinushka and I triple-checked his bag to make sure we'd packed everything he needed. I would drop him off by 3 p.m. and picked him up at 10 a.m. the following day. As soon as we pulled up to Karl's rented house, Jonathan shouted the word *no*, as if he already knew we were leaving him there.

The house told a story of neglect, the front yard with no grass, the screen door tattered from overuse. I carried Jonathan to the doorstep, his guttural cries heart-wrenching. My hand was shaking and my heart racing as I knocked hard.

"It's okay. We will be back before you know it," I said. "We love you very much, and we will be here in the morning." I knew I was failing to reassure him.

The door slowly opened. Karl peeked his head out as if he were expecting someone else. Behind him stood his common-law wife, her exhausted expression telegraphing that she'd given up the fight, too. She was tall and very thin, with a high bun, a fading hairline, and missing teeth. I couldn't help but stare. Another woman's child would be sleeping in her home, and her bulging eyes narrowed in on Jonathan with poorly concealed resentment.

"Pink! Why does my son have on pink socks?" Karl suddenly yelled angrily.

The polite Karl from the mediation proceedings was gone. He smelled heavily of alcohol, and his sickening desire to show us that he was "the man" had returned.

"They're just pink because I washed them with the colored laundry," I offered in the same fearful, hushed tone I imagined his wife used. In Karl's eyes, his son would be gay because of pink socks. Again, I felt his dislike of my relationship with Dinushka.

I began to loosen my grip on Jonathan, working up the courage to actually hand him over. Dinushka stood just steps behind me, ready to catch me if I fell. We both kissed Jonathan on the forehead and then let him go. He reached out to us—scared, tearful, and uncertain of what would come next.

Dinushka and I walked back to the car carrying our heavy guilt and fear. I could see the goose bumps on the back of Dinushka's neck as she gave Karl and his wife one last look. We spent that night at Uncle Main's house, too worried to get much sleep but barely talking, counting the hours until we would get Jonathan back.

THE NEXT MORNING, we were on Karl's doorstep again. I felt sick to my stomach, half-afraid Jonathan had had a great time, further complicating our situation, and half-afraid of the opposite—that he'd been hurt in some way. As Karl opened the door, the smell of cigarette smoke met me before he did. Jonathan was in the same clothes we'd dropped him off in, his diaper heavy from not being changed. It looked like he hadn't been bathed either. Orange Cheetos dust surrounded his mouth. His eyes were bloodshot from crying. I took him in my arms and noticed his clothes reeked of smoke.

"He didn't want to eat much. He stood on the couch for most of the evening, looking out the window," Karl said, rubbing his head. "Thanks for bringing him. I'll see you next time." He gave Jonathan a smile.

As soon as we got into the car, I rolled down all the windows, because I couldn't deal with the smell. When we put Jonathan in the car seat, we told him how much we missed him and then surprised him with his favorite doughnuts from Dunkin'. Our normally noisy and inquisitive child refused to speak but gobbled down the treats like he hadn't touched food for a week.

Before we hit the Long Island Expressway, I pulled over to change Jonathan's diaper and clothes. When I went into the bag, everything smelled like smoke. I had told Karl about Jonathan's breathing problems, that smoke could cause an episode that would require a nebulizer—a small machine connected with a mask to Jonathan's face, providing medication to help him breathe. It didn't make sense to change him out of one pair of smoke-filled clothes and into another. I put his jacket in the trunk to lessen the smell and focused on changing his diaper, so he could be at least a bit more comfortable on the two-hour drive home.

"How did you sleep?" Dinushka asked Jonathan.

He didn't say anything.

"What did you have for dinner?" I asked.

Nothing.

"Where did you sleep?" she asked.

Silence.

For the rest of the ride, he stared out the window.

When we got home, we filled up the tub with bubbles and gave Jonathan a warm bath.

He still wouldn't talk to us. Where was the same secure little boy we'd dropped off the night before?

The following morning, I got in touch with Child Protective Services and asked the visits to end due to neglect and abuse.

"It's only one visit," the rep said. "He hasn't been treated like this long enough for it to be called neglect. His father is trying, and we are helping to educate him."

All I could think was: *Who is going to help Jonathan? Don't his needs and feelings matter more than anyone else's?* I felt defeated, powerless, and scared while I listened to this stranger tell me what was best for my son.

"So we just call you back if it gets worse?" I asked.

"Yes, that's correct. Once we receive the report of neglect, we have twenty-four hours to contact you and get the specifics of what happened. From there, we have sixty days to investigate. Once the investigation is over, we will then say it was 'indicated'—that neglect did happen—or it was 'unfounded' and neglect did not occur."

After a week and a half of getting Jonathan back to normal,

we had to prepare for the second overnight visit. This time, we met Karl at a mall a little closer to the Bronx, where he showed up in a car filled with smoke. Jonathan began to scream and shout uncontrollably as soon as he saw him approach. Grabbing our arms, his nails digging into our skin, Jonathan begged Dinushka and me not to let him go. We held back our own tears as his gushed uncontrollably.

After Karl pulled him into the car, Jonathan threw up because he'd been crying for so long. He could sense his father's anger, withdrawing as Karl yelled at him. As the car pulled off with Jonathan inside, we could still hear his cries, and I wept in Dinushka's arms.

The next day, Jonathan was again returned to us smelling of smoke, famished, and silent. Dinushka got on her knees that night and told God she couldn't stand this injustice being done to Jonathan, being done to us. This was a new side of Dinushka I'd not seen before. She was filled with anger. She'd later tell me that she was willing to sell her soul to the devil if it meant stopping Karl from doing more harm to Jonathan.

God heard her prayers.

16

————

THE NEXT TIME Jonathan was supposed to spend the weekend at his father's house, he came down with a cold so severe his airway passages were blocked. He required frequent treatments from his nebulizer to open his lungs. I called his father on Friday to tell him.

"I know Jonathan is supposed to have an overnight visit with you this weekend, but he is very sick."

Silence.

"I think it's best that he doesn't come so he doesn't get worse."

"Okay, I understand," Karl said, though it was clear he didn't. I imagined him gritting his teeth in anger, but he said, "Give him a kiss for me and tell him I love him."

As the sunshine began to peek through the windows early the next day, my phone rang. It was my cousin Natasha, calling to tell me that Karl's house had been raided by the police the night before. Karl's teenage sons had been accused of breaking into the homes of their neighbors, and one of those neighbors happened to be a cop. When they searched Karl's home, they found stolen guns underneath the bed Jonathan would have been sleeping in—and the guns were loaded.

Two of Karl's sons, his two daughters, and his wife were all taken into police custody, and Karl's grandchildren—two little girls—were placed in the temporary care of Child Protective Services. Dinushka and I were also questioned by CPS. They even searched through our Bronx apartment.

"Karl was supposed to have Jonathan in his care that night," the CPS caseworker said. "This means that all the kids associated with the home in question must be deemed safe. Jonathan's safety is what we are investigating here."

Being under investigation ourselves was infuriating— Dinushka and I thought it was a complete waste of everyone's time and emotions when we all knew what the end result would be. We were eventually cleared of any kind of neglect or abuse. But it felt so degrading and unfair, not to mention a waste of time for the CPS workers.

After the ordeal, I wrote to our state senators and then to our governor. I wanted them to know the battle I was fighting and asked them to take a look at the foster care and adoption laws in the state of New York. They all wrote back with a form letter: *Thank you for writing to me. I hear how challenging this situation is. I encourage you to reach out to your local officials.* None of them offered any guidance or help.

Since the court order had gone into effect, Jonathan had only slept over at his father's house twice. After the police raid, he never did again. A few days after the raid, Karl and I came to a new agreement outside of court and without any legal mediation. I agreed to trips to Long Island every two weeks—all expenses footed by Dinushka and me, a small price to pay to ensure that Jonathan was safe—while Dinushka and I would remain present at every visit, hovering in the background while Karl tried to build a relationship with his son.

TWO WEEKS AFTER the incident, we visited my grandparents in Virginia for Valentine's Day weekend. Knowing the tension we'd been living with, they gave us the gift of a date night at an Italian restaurant not far from their home. As we walked toward the entrance, I slipped my hand into the pocket of my black peacoat, making sure that the little box was still there. Inside was a white gold promise ring with four tiny diamonds.

"You can't propose to me first," Dinushka had told me during one of our many conversations about marriage. "I have to be the one."

But I wanted to give her the ring for Valentine's Day. Lately, she'd been asking me a lot of questions, needing reassurance. "Are you sure you want to be with me?" she would ask. "Do you think you'd ever want to be with a man?" I think Dinushka was concerned that my wanting more children, my wanting to experience giving birth, indicated a desire for a heteronormative life.

"If I wanted to be with a man, I would be. Besides it's sorta hard to be with a man if you're a lesbian," I'd joke.

The ring was meant to be a signal that my love and my life would be promised to her. I was unsure how she would take it. Would she accept it? Would she reject it? Would she think it was a proposal? I knew how we felt about each other. I knew that the love we had was strong. I wasn't scared to hand her the box with the ring in it. But I also knew that we had so much stacked against us: coming out, cultural differences, custody issues, and more.

"Should I give you my gift now?" I asked while we waited for our table.

"Gift? I thought we weren't doing gifts!" She pushed back one of her black curls and I could see the worry on her face.

"I know, but I wanted to. I want you to take my gift and wear it. I am giving it to you because I love you a lot. I am giving you this gift because I am promising you my love." I handed her the box. "I know you said not to propose to you first, so this is not a proposal. This is a promise."

She opened the box and gasped. "A promise ring? What are you promising?"

"I am promising you myself. You don't need to ever worry. My heart will always and forever be with you. I love you, Dinushka."

She put the ring on her finger and then screamed, "We're engaged!"

"No, we are not engaged," I insisted. My heart was racing; my breath felt frozen in my chest. "I have promised you all of me."

"That's what a proposal is, Nik. If your heart is always and forever with me, then you're saying you want to spend the rest of your life with me, right?"

"Well, yes, but . . ."

She wasn't wrong. But the word *marriage*, the act of marriage, scared me. People in my life left. Rarely did anyone stay.

Now, I was sitting across from the woman who everything felt right with, the person who'd showed up for me before I'd even known I needed anyone. I had someone who loved me, nurtured me, gave me all of her, and made me want to be better than I was. She'd welcomed a son into her life not knowing if he would ever truly be hers.

Dinushka placed her hand against her cheek. The diamonds, though small, sparkled underneath the lights. "How does it look?"

"It looks perfect," I said.

DINUSHKA'S PROPOSAL CAME a few weeks later, on an unseasonably warm March day. The three of us had driven out to Connecticut to stay at her parents' house. Each winter, her mom and dad packed up and went to their homeland of Sri Lanka for a few months, leaving Dinushka to take care of their house while they were away, and they were gone now. Though they were still struggling to come to terms with our relationship, and with Jonathan, they were getting there. And Dinushka had told them about the ring.

After we arrived, we took a walk in downtown Stamford, pushing Jonathan in his light-blue stroller. Oblivious to what Dinushka had planned, I followed her as she made left and right turns, each step filled with intention.

She led me to a small staircase that ran along the outside of the cinema. I held on to the metal rail, and together we took each step, planting our feet on the concrete and dragging the stroller along. Opposite the rail, to my left, were brightly colored sculptures of abstract art. We made it to the bottom stair, and she asked me to sit down. She began to speak, and I felt my body change. This was my dream, to be hers for the rest of my life.

"I love you very much. I finally found the perfect ring for you. I was still searching when you proposed. It's an antique from the 1920s, an art deco style. The seller said it was worn by a merchant's wife, who probably never took it off. You can tell from the state of the ring the woman was a hard worker. I will eventually replace the diamond in the middle before our wedding day. I hope you like it. Nikkya Hargrove, will you marry me?"

I didn't scream as she had when I'd given her the promise ring, but the smile on my face said it all. I looked down at the white gold band and admired the diamond solitaire with two side stones. She had bought the wedding band and the engagement ring as a set. I had never seen a style like this, and I loved it. We were each other's forever. This was it.

Of course, the bliss of our engagement did not protect us from being tied to the custody agreement. The rings we now wore were not only outward signs of the love we had for each other, but also the promise to endure the further battles we knew were coming.

Though we were engaged in 2009, same-sex marriage would not become legally recognized across the United States until June 26, 2015. Connecticut would recognize our union as a civil one, though, via a law adopted by the state in 2005. This meant we would have more protections there. It also meant that in a court, our marriage would be just as valid as anyone else's.

Newly engaged, we had no idea what kind of discrimination we'd face along the way as a (one day) married couple.

THE VISITS WITH Karl continued.

For the next four years, every other weekend we drove those two hours each way to meet Karl, usually at work, where we'd spend the morning walking around every inch of the aquarium. Sometimes he would be with us, but usually not. To win Jonathan's affection, Karl would give him a toy or a stuffed animal from the aquarium's arcade. We'd buy lunch in the cafeteria, filling our bellies with food that comforted more than nourished, checking out emotionally from the experience of being in a place with a person we didn't want to be with.

We all tired quickly of watching the seal feedings every couple hours, looking at the sharks, and the incessant announcements in cheerfully robotic voices. After popping in to see the penguins and watching the fish swim about in the koi pond, we were ready to leave. We mostly walked around outside, where Jonathan could roam freely without bumping into anyone or us having to run after him.

When Karl lost his job, we didn't go to the aquarium anymore; instead, we took Jonathan to see Karl at his home. Karl and his family moved frequently, from one rented house to another. Every visit was tense, and Jonathan could feel it. He was attentive, his eyes wide and occasionally darting from mine, Dinushka's, and then to his father's. His tiny hand grasped mine tightly during those visits, as if he was afraid we'd leave him there alone again.

We were polite, but underneath the pleasantries, we were all angry. Dinushka was upset because she couldn't protect Jonathan. One time at the aquarium, she had witnessed him in the parking lot giving someone something and taking something in return. It looked sketchy to her. "He just did that in broad daylight while he was supposed to be working," she told me.

I was enraged at every visit because this was now our life. We drove long distances only to see Karl mostly ignore Jonathan.

Karl was angry, I assumed, because two women—two lesbians—were raising his son, and maybe because I'd turned down his offer to take me out to dinner all those months ago.

It was Karl's temper that erupted one fall Saturday afternoon while we were at his latest rental house. He was washing his car and asked Jonathan to help. "Every man needs to learn how to take care of his car," he said, his chest puffed. It was chilly outside, and I was always vigilant about Jonathan's breathing, not wanting his cough to come back.

"I don't really want him to get wet, because he doesn't have another pair of clothes," I said.

Karl flew into a rage. "If I want to wash the fuckin' car—*my* car, with *my* son—I will do it. Neither of you can say a damn thing about it."

Jonathan hid behind the car to cry. Then he wiped his tears on his shirt, straightened up, and walked over to his dad. "Come on, Dad. I can help you," he said, defusing the situation with his small, strong voice.

These forced visits were at least better than having Jonathan sleep over alone at his father's house. Dinushka and I believed he deserved to know who his biological father was, so we tried to give Karl a chance.

The way Karl chose to raise his kids and the predicament he found himself in made me feel both infuriated with and sorry for him. When he eventually revealed some of the traumas he experienced as a child—being bullied by classmates, stories of crime, the death of someone he loved—I felt for him. He tried to remedy his emotional ups and downs with alcohol. But his mood swings would impact every visit for years to come.

We never knew which Karl we would get: the easygoing Karl who would go with the flow, the irate Karl who could not be pacified by small talk, or the detached Karl, barely speaking to anyone, just watching the television. Dinushka and I left every single visit frustrated with our predicament.

Over the next several years, Jonathan got to know his father—the good, the bad, and the ugly. He would have memories of him as he grew up, but also memories of the life Dinushka and I had created with him. My mother had made countless promises to me that she could never keep: *I'll see you tomorrow. I'll call you again later. When I get clean, we will be a family again.* She'd even broken promises to herself, like when she started high school and never finished, or the time she tried to become a nurse's aide. And though my mother had wanted to regain custody of Jonathan, she could never have provided the life that Dinushka and I were giving him.

Sometimes it felt like if there was any silver lining during those visits, it was that I only had to protect Jonathan from one of his biological parents, not both.

MY FRIEND LAUREN came with me during one of our Christmas visits to Karl's house. Jonathan was still quite young then. Dinushka had to be with her family, and Lauren volunteered to act as my protection, and as eyes and ears witnessing what we were going through. She asked questions during the drive, trying to predict what it would be like when we got there.

"Should I come in with you or wait in the car?" she asked.

"What do you want to do?"

"Whatever you think is best. Do you think he will have gifts for Jonathan?"

"I don't know what to think about this guy anymore," I said.

When we pulled up in my car, there was a small, sparse-looking wreath hanging precariously on the front door. I looked back at Jonathan sitting in his booster seat and wondered what he was thinking.

"Jonathan, do you know we're at your dad's house?" I asked.

Silence.

"Mommy and Lauren will be here with you," I reassured him.

Silence.

I parked on the street, leaving my old Ford Focus in plain sight. We all moved haltingly, not wanting to begin the short walk to the front door.

When it opened, we were met with that familiar smell of cigarette smoke, along with the sight of Karl's wife. I caught a pained smile on her face as she said hello. Lauren trailed behind us, her head low, looking around the room every so often. The two of us sat down, side by side, on the frayed blue-and-white striped couch, Jonathan on my right knee.

"Come over here, Jonathan," Karl commanded.

Jonathan walked the few feet to reach the couch where his father sat across from us, but his legs moved slowly, his corduroy pants whooshing with each stiff step, as if he did not want to get any closer.

"I got something for you," Karl said.

Jonathan's face betrayed how curious he was about what it could be. Karl left the living room and came back with a huge box, wrapped in shiny silver wrapping paper. "Here, Jonathan, this is for you," he said, smiling. "Open it."

Inside the box was a toy electric guitar, with buttons that when pushed would play "I Love Rock 'n' Roll" over and over.

By the time we ended our two-hour visit, I was ready to get rid of it.

Karl's gift reminded me of the gifts my father had sent me from Germany when I was a kid. In the US Army, stationed abroad, he would send presents to prove that he'd thought of me. Once, he sent me a delicate yellow-gold-and-diamond bracelet. When it arrived, I smiled for days, grateful to know he'd put something for me in the mail.

The reality, though, was that he felt like a ghost.

Like the gifts I held on to from my father, Jonathan held on to that guitar for years. I don't know if he thought about his father when he played it, as I did when I wore the bracelet my father had given me.

We spent four Christmases in Karl's various houses, and he never invited us past the kitchen or living room. But truthfully, we didn't want to see more of his temporary spaces than we had to. We didn't even ask to use the bathroom, because we didn't want to leave each other alone with him or his family. We needed to be witness to the words exchanged, remain on guard, ready at a moment's notice to make our exit together. We each carried a change of clothes with us—it was the only way to get rid of the smoke smell—and declined his invitations to partake of his store-bought meals.

We were always anxious about unexpected visitors who knocked at Karl's door, fearful for our safety. We didn't know who Karl hung out with besides his kids and his wife. And I was always thinking that this would be the visit when the cops would once again raid his home. One visit, we did meet Karl's younger brother, who arrived on his motorcycle. With no helmet for either of them, he said to Jonathan, "Hey, little man, let's go for a ride," and before Dinushka or I could say a word, he had positioned Jonathan in front of him and left, the exhaust lingering long after they made their way down the street.

My chest was on fire, the terror burning from the inside out. I looked at Dinushka, her mouth open, words frozen inside. But before we'd had a chance to fully digest what had just happened right in front of us, the complete disregard for Jonathan's safety and for what we—as his parents—wanted, they were back and both in one piece.

That same brother shared stories of his own childhood trauma with us, maybe as a way of bonding, maybe as a way of scaring us. "I carry a gun with me," he told us. "When I was little, I saw a man get shot, point-blank, right there in the corner store near our house. Since then, I don't leave home without my gun."

DINUSHKA AND I tried to make our own Christmases—before and after our visits with Karl—as memorable and happy for Jonathan as we could. We'd race from Long Island to Connecticut to spend what was left of the holiday with her family, an experience that showed Jonathan how different life could be. The moment our car pulled into their driveway, the front door opened and we were met with hellos and hugs.

"You must be hungry. Come, come," her father would say as we took off our shoes and jackets.

Dinushka's family had finally come to a place of acceptance. Even though they were still adjusting to the reality of us as lesbians and the complications of our custody situation with Jonathan, they were helping us define what family was all about: commitment, honesty, and trust. It was in Dinushka's family's home that we opened our Christmas gifts together. It was at their table that we sat down for Christmas dinner, with loud chatter filling the room along with the aroma of her mother's lamb chops, a recipe she'd read about in the latest issue of *Martha Stewart Living*.

Jonathan would run off and play with Dinushka's nephew, Ishan. They'd quickly become best friends. Ishan helped Jonathan adjust to the newness of everything—the loud family gatherings and eventually all the questions that would come his way. Ishan and Jonathan first met when Dinushka and her brother got together for a playdate at the Bronx Zoo. She shared with me that she'd had nervous cramps in her stomach as she waited in anticipation to see how Jonathan would react to her brother and her nephew. The kids' immediate connection was uncanny. They reached out to each other, their small brown hands locking as her brother carried Ishan on his shoulders and Dinushka carried Jonathan on hers. The joy that radiated from their tiny hearts at Christmas helped the adults around them see what mattered most (and the great many knock-knock jokes they told made every get-together an immense pleasure).

I'd once worried about how I'd fit into a home that was so culturally and socially different from my own, but I gave Dinushka's family all of me regardless: a Black woman, raising her half brother as her son, brought up by my grandparents because my mother was addicted to crack cocaine and had spent time in jail. I had no savings account that my parents had funded for me, no secure financial foundation to build my future on, and yet I never felt out of place when I was with them. They welcomed me, offering me a glass of wine or a cup of tea with dessert, even worked hard to learn how to pronounce my name.

They were trying, and that's what mattered to me.

17

DINUSHKA HAD SUCH a strong connection to Jonathan. They spoke their own language, and their playful banter solidified her role as the fun parent. They joked about farts. They would build and rebuild trains and houses with Jonathan's Legos. They would run around the apartment and have impromptu dance parties. Even when Jonathan was silent, Dinushka could sense what he needed.

"I understand his soul," she would say.

Jonathan was only eleven months old when they met and three years old when she began to feel like she wanted him to call her something other than Di-Di, something with more meaning. It felt organic, natural when he began to call her Mom, and by then, she embraced it.

As Jonathan became more verbal at four years old, he told us that he no longer wanted to go to Long Island to visit his father. He always had stomachaches whenever we got in the car to drive to Karl's house. Dinushka encouraged him to not be afraid to talk, to show his emotions with his father.

"I don't want to visit on the weekends," he finally told Karl, words that could not be misinterpreted or twisted, words that Karl needed to hear. What Dinushka and I had said over the years hadn't mattered to Karl, but we hoped hearing from Jonathan would be different.

"Is that right?" Karl asked, unable to mask his skepticism, his suspicion that Jonathan had been coached, but taking it in nonetheless.

Not much later, I told Karl, "We'd like to leave New York and move to Connecticut for better schools." Jonathan would soon be five, and we wanted to be in a better neighborhood. My words caught him by surprise, the wrinkles in his forehead tight as he processed this information. "Your visits would remain the same. We'd still drive Jonathan out," I continued.

After a minute or so, he responded with a simple "All right."

And that's all we needed to put the wheels in motion. Relocating made sense for Dinushka and me, but it was mostly for Jonathan, who would begin preschool in the fall. I kept my promise to Karl, still making the now two-and-half-hour drive out to Long Island, keeping our twice-a-month visits. With each visit, Karl, never very attentive, seemed less interested in engaging with us or Jonathan. When Jonathan had to use the bathroom, Karl would not offer to take him. When Jonathan wanted to play, Karl would not hop on a swing with him.

IN CONNECTICUT, DINUSHKA'S father helped us find an apartment just a five-minute car ride from their home. Since he'd retired from his job as a financial analyst, he'd taken up real estate as a diversion, a suggestion from his wife, who was also retired. Real estate kept him busy and out of her hair so they didn't get on each other's nerves. He would find listings, call or email Dinushka about them, and then we would discuss.

The second-floor apartment in a split-level house, above a young couple with no kids, seemed perfect. It was within walking distance of the train, ten minutes to the grocery store, and in a good school district. There was even a little fast-food restaurant nearby, known for its hot dogs and its fried Oreos.

Once we moved in, I began to think about our wedding: Should we set a date? What would the ideal time of year be? What kind of theme should we have? My questions, though frequent, were appropriate for someone who was engaged to be married. But Dinushka didn't handle change well. So in an effort to get the ball rolling, I began to purchase wedding magazines. I left one on our coffee table and another on my nightstand. I'd turn to a page in a wedding magazine and ask, "What do you think of this dress?" Always concerned about our finances, Dinushka would respond by wondering whether or not we had saved enough yet.

Eventually, we agreed to get married in two years, and with 2011 in mind, I began to really plan our wedding in earnest, vision boards and all. Thinking about the day gave me something to look forward to—I threw myself into it.

EVEN AS OUR job titles changed over the years, our incomes had not climbed very much. Fortunately, the Connecticut state government had enacted a subsidy program helping low- to moderate-income families afford preschool, and it had published the guidelines and parameters necessary to qualify. We applied for and received the aid. The assistance wasn't much, but it was better than nothing at all.

I'd always loved school. I'd thought it was a gift to get the chance every September to try again, a clean slate to do better than the year before. Every year, I'd go back-to-school shopping with Nanny and Aunt She-She, and my mood would lift. Seeing aisles and aisles of nice, neatly arranged backpacks and notebooks made me so happy. For me, there was so much promise in showing up each day to learn something new. School was my safe place, and I wanted Jonathan to love it as much as I had.

Dinushka had grown up disliking school. She'd been teased by her elementary school peers because of her ethnic differences, and for the way she looked. She would spend hours after school doing homework, trying to keep up, but she was forgetful and easily distracted, finding it challenging to consistently stay focused. After her hard work, and in the face of her parents' denials, she was finally diagnosed with attention deficit disorder. Partly for this reason, Dinushka and I fell on different sides of the first-day-of-school excitement, and we had opposite ideas of how Jonathan would handle an academic setting.

Forever the optimist, I was hopeful that he would learn to enjoy the classroom and make friends. Jonathan had been in day care before entering a traditional preschool setting, so being around kids and teachers was not new to him. But Dinushka was a self-professed realist and we had already seen some issues around Jonathan's attention and anxiety. She went into the school year fearful that it would be much like it was for her: socially challenging and academically difficult.

She was right.

We'd decided to get married in 2011, and that year, as Jonathan began kindergarten, I started planning our wedding. Because Jonathan's birthday fell in November, he began that September as one of the youngest in his class. Before his seat was warm in his new kindergarten classroom, the phone calls from his teacher began. Each call from Jonathan's teacher began the same way. She'd tell us he was okay and not hurt, and then she'd tell us what had happened. He had growled at other kids, or he had spent the morning hiding under the table, or he had failed to engage with toys at playtime.

I was not prepared for these reports, but Dinushka was not at all surprised. She had taken a new position as the administrative assistant at an Episcopal church, but as a former teacher, she was ready to make an action plan. I thought Jonathan needed more time to develop, though, that he was young and still figuring out who he was. She'd need to convince me that something needed fixing.

The year before, when Jonathan was in preschool, his teacher told us that she loved all her students, "even the bad ones." Dinushka and I were both stunned and hurt. We worried that her perception of Jonathan as a "bad one" meant that she was treating him differently in the classroom. I wanted to scream at her that she should not be a teacher if she could not handle *all* her students. I wanted her to know that Jonathan was not a bad kid. Instead, I said nothing. Instead, I nodded my head. But my hackles were up.

At check-ins with the after-school staff at his new school,

meetings that became a frequent part of our schedules, we discussed his behaviors. I didn't want to believe that he had a short attention span or that his constant talking or inability to sit through dinner meant anything. Deep down, I knew I was not being totally honest with myself. But I was having a hard time coming to grips with it, even as I witnessed his behavior.

When I went to pick up Jonathan from school, I'd watch other children on the playground—how they'd interact not only with other kids but also with their parents. Jonathan sometimes found it difficult to communicate with us and didn't engage with anyone on the playground. Dinushka was always willing to play games with him, but he would easily become frustrated, often throwing his Legos instead of building things.

"Something is going on," Ms. Pellet, his kindergarten teacher, told us. "He struggles with occupying himself, using his own imagination, and sitting through a lesson,"

Ms. Pellet stood shorter than my own five-foot frame, her hair in a pixie cut, with longer bangs resting on the side of her face. Her clothes were fabulous, and her glasses often changed to match her attire. She'd been teaching at this same school for over forty years and had seen lots of different types of students. Ms. Pellet suggested we reach out to the school's occupational therapist to see if she could help with Jonathan's restlessness. The occupational therapist provided Jonathan with leg bands that could be strapped to his chair, giving him tension, which helped channel any anxiety or pent-up energy. She also recommended a weighted backpack to build his muscles, along with the stamina to get him through the day.

I wanted Jonathan to have a normal social life, to have connections with kids and playdates that turned into friendships, ones he could be grateful for as he grew older. Most of all, I wanted to protect him from the emotional and physical stress of being the keeper of secrets. I knew what that felt like.

FOR JONATHAN'S FIFTH birthday, we invited his entire kindergarten class to our neighborhood park. There was lots of space for running around, two different playgrounds, a tennis court, and a skate park. We hoped the kids who came would have a good time and we'd get to know their parents.

We decorated the wooden picnic tables not too far from Jonathan's favorite playground. We ordered pepperoni pizza, his favorite. We bought a vanilla sheet cake with buttercream frosting and *Happy Birthday, Jonathan!* written on it in green, his favorite color.

Jonathan's preschool friend Gabriel arrived first. Then his cousin, Ishan. Next, my best friend Diana's soon-to-be-five-year-old son, Luc. They all were ready to celebrate. But where were the children from his kindergarten class? We'd received no calls or texts from parents letting us know they wouldn't be joining us. After thirty minutes, Dinushka and I began to worry.

Jonathan had once mentioned to Dinushka that some kids thought it was weird that he had two moms. What was really weird was that there was only one other mother who had made an effort to talk with us. We just hoped they would let kids be kids, and not let their preconceived notions about what they believed a family should look like interfere. Our eyes darted from one side of the park to see if a child, any child, had a wrapped birthday gift in their hands.

Not one child from his kindergarten class ever arrived.

Dinushka and I knew his kindergarten teacher and the other parents were mostly on the conservative side, that we were the only same-sex couple in the school, and a Black and brown couple to boot. We, of course, couldn't know 100 percent that the reason for their absence was due to who our family was or because of Jonathan's inability to connect with other children. In any case, Dinushka and I felt sick about it.

After that, we became more deliberate about the environments where we introduced our family. We gravitated toward more liberal spaces, including our local Jewish community center. We started a gay and lesbian families group on Facebook. We knew we would have to continue to work hard to find our village. And we did.

Eventually, our circle would include all different kinds of families, queer and not. These were people we could reach out to, bounce questions off of, go to when we encountered parenting problems. These are the parents who did, and still do, help us navigate the absence of a checkbox on a form that does not make room for us.

18

JONATHAN WAS ONE of the reasons we decided to get married. We wanted a foundation for him that was solid, and never wanted him to worry about our family changing. We were in this thing for the long haul, and our marriage would show him that. We'd chosen one another.

I knew the process of getting married would not be easy for a Black and a brown woman. We were bringing together two very different cultures, families, and histories. Though Dinushka had had fears, the wedding had become important to us both. Neither of us had been little girls who dreamed of walking down the aisle, fantasizing about the kind of dress we'd wear or what color the flowers would be. Maybe because early on we both knew we were queer and because our families and society told us that queer people could not or should not be married.

But now we were both excited—and a little scared. We'd never in our lives planned something so big, with so much riding on it. This was our wedding, and we were most definitely setting the stage for how our families would see us for years to come. We wanted them to see who we truly were—two queer parents who were building a family on love and with God's blessing.

We hired a wedding planner, someone who could help us navigate all the moving pieces. Tall, with a gray beard and sharp eyes, Gary was a force to be reckoned with. He had a fiery, to-the-point kind of way about him and no time to waste, and he was quick to dismiss an idea that he'd known from his years of experience simply would not work.

Gary made me nervous. He'd throw a "No" out quickly and then be on to the next decision. But he was the expert, and in his eyes, we were paying him to tell us what to do—and also, of course, to take care of us, hear us, walk with us. And Gary understood our story from a personal perspective: older and from a more conservative generation than ours, he had come out late in life and knew our battles.

"Whatever she wants," Dinushka told Gary at our first meeting, only partly joking. It was easy for Dinushka to keep up with Gary. Her mother had the same kind of type-A personality. She knew who she was and what she wanted, and she wasn't afraid to speak her mind. I considered my interactions with Gary practice for future conversations with my mother-in-law.

One afternoon, Gary arranged for us to look at flowers in Manhattan so he could get a real-life sense of our taste. Dinushka was unable to take off from work, so she instead suggested I ask her mom to come along. "It'll be a nice time for you to get to know who my mother is," she said.

I am sensitive and can become paralyzed by the smallest

criticism. So Dinushka tried to prepare me before every Sri Lankan family gathering. "Don't get upset if she says something about whatever it is you're wearing," she said. "She may not like any of the flowers you like. Be ready to answer personal questions. Just be yourself. Remember, I've already chosen you—there's no need to impress anyone."

I was far from fashionable and mildly colorblind, so Dinushka had helped me pick out an outfit for the occasion. Beautiful and confident, Dinushka's mother, Rohini, was always dressed in clothes that made me question my own wardrobe. She matched from head to toe, with even her earrings appropriately coordinated. For our trip to New York, she wore a salva, a colorful dress with matching pants common in South Asian cultures. Out of respect, I called her Aunty.

As my mother-in-law and I sat together on the train into the city, we chatted. She asked questions about the wedding, and I realized it was bittersweet doing this with her instead of with my own mother. I was attempting to make new memories with Rohini since I'd never get to make them with Lisa. When we hopped off and made our way through Manhattan, Rohini led the way. She'd ridden that train so many times before, for her job as the deputy director of human resources for UNICEF, and she was the perfect navigator.

It turns out Dinushka had misjudged her mother. She didn't ask me any intrusive questions and kept the conversation light. Still, by the time we made it to meet Gary, I was exhausted from the walking, and from the anticipatory fear that I'd need to answer something I wasn't ready for. Something like "Why did your mom decide to do drugs instead of taking care of her children?"

Halfway through our flower-shopping trip, Gary was getting a sense of what both my mother-in-law and I liked. Rohini had pointed to long yellow plants with small yellow balls growing from them—budding coconut trees, picked too early to grow full coconuts. They didn't appeal to me, and I knew they wouldn't to Dinushka either.

"If there's something you don't like and she keeps pushing it, or something you know I wouldn't like, call me. I will handle her," Dinushka had instructed.

I phoned Dinushka to let her know that I was surviving but that her mother was insisting on coconut plants. I could tell by the look on Rohini's face that she expected a decision in the next few minutes, her eyes boring through me like Nanny's did when I wasn't paying attention in church. I held my breath, waiting for Dinushka's response, second-guessing if I knew her as well as I thought I did.

"I can just imagine what they look like. We don't need them," she said, responding just as Aunt Lady would have, to the point and without hesitation.

"Well, I think they maybe could be a nice addition as we walk down the aisle," I said, fearful of diverging from the "pleasant Nikkya" script and not wanting to rock the boat. Plus I knew Dinushka's mom was listening to our conversation.

"Dinushka, you can put them on the railing. It'll give the wedding a little Sri Lankan flare," Rohini said, loud enough for Dinushka to hear.

"How much will this cost us?" Dinushka wanted to know.

"Well, your mom said she would pay for them," I said.

"No, Nik. I don't want the coconut plants," Dinushka replied and then hung up.

The coconut plants would end up decorating the front steps of our reception. This foreshadowed the kind of relationship I'd continue to have with my mother-in-law, one in which I would more often than not accept her taste and maintain some peace between her and Dinushka.

Still, over the course of the planning of our wedding, my mother in-law and I became closer than I'd anticipated. My work in those early days was to show Dinushka's parents that my mother's choices were not a reflection on me, to show them how devoted I was to their daughter and would be for the rest of her life. In turn, Rohini worked hard to get to know me, for me. With each step toward the altar, my confidence in myself grew and I feared other people's judgments less.

Sometimes, I still wonder what flowers my mom would have chosen if she had been walking among them with us that day.

19

——

LEADING UP TO our wedding, Dinushka continued prepping me for any potential intrusive questions I could get from the aunties and uncles. There were any number of gatherings before the big day, and Dinushka warned that the aunties might critique both my makeup and my fashion in one breath. We weren't close enough yet for them to comment on my weight, but I learned that a simple "She would look great in a saree" was code for "Her hips and bum are well-rounded, and her bust small enough for the top." She also cautioned me that the uncles might want to know where I stood on national issues and what my education was. And it was true that I was unable to avoid a few political discussions in which I was grilled on my opinions about which presidential candidate was the most fiscally conservative or which political party should go kick dirt.

When Dinushka would visit my aunts and uncles with me, they'd ask me "Aren't you done eating yet?" or "Aren't you full?" whenever I attempted to fill my plate a second time. I knew they wanted to include Dinushka in their judgments, too. She would tell Nanny how good the chicken was and then lick all ten of her fingers. She was full of compliments on the collards. She ate my grandmother's food like it gave her real comfort, just as her father's chicken curry gave me.

My family listened to Dinushka's stories about her life, though mostly they wanted her to listen to theirs. They didn't know where Sri Lanka was, and her repeating "It's a South Asian country just below India" helped them become slightly more aware of other parts of the world.

"So you're Indian?" Uncle Wayne would ask.

"That's actually a different country with a different language, but we share similarities," she'd say.

"So you're Indian?" Uncle Wayne would ask again, still confused.

"Um, sure, close to it."

Dinushka liked my family. They offered her beer and laughed out loud with her. She even got to talk about her favorite subject with Nanny: Jesus.

SOON THE REHEARSAL dinner night was upon us. Our friends and family packed into the living room of Dinushka's parents' house, a room that once felt big but was now crowded with at least twenty-five people. On the back deck there were chairs and tables, and a big tent was set up for dinner. We all stood, shoulder to shoulder, so close that I could see the sweat beads on the foreheads of just about everyone. It was hot, and we were packed into Dinushka's parents' house. When we had all gathered,

Dinushka's dad pulled a neatly folded piece of white paper out of his shirt pocket:

"Khalil Gibran said that parents are the bows through which arrows are sent out. We cannot hold on to our children but instead let them go, and now the time has come to let Dinushka go. She has been a kind, loving, caring, and thoughtful child, and she has found an equally kind, loving, caring, and thoughtful partner in Nikkya." He went on. "Love has no barriers, and it can break all traditions. It is not easy to break traditions, and it requires courage to do so. I admire the courage of Dinushka."

His words erased any doubts I had about where I stood in his family. I knew in my heart that I was accepted and welcomed. After his speech, Dinushka's parents both embraced me and gave me a watch to symbolize that we would be entering into this new time as a family.

As the night came to an end, my eyes were red and I was exhausted. Dinushka and I slept apart, she at her parents' house and me at our apartment with my grandparents and Jonathan. I lay in our bed alone, thinking about our wedding the next day, when she would be beside me, no longer my fiancée but my wife. I thought about how wonderful it would be to have my grandparents right there with me, supporting me on my trip down the aisle.

I looked up at the ceiling, thinking about how the ring on my finger would soon have a wedding band accompanying it. As I began to drift off to sleep, I reflected on how proud of myself I was—that I'd stayed the course, that I hadn't let my own fear of abandonment take me away from the person who had promised me forever.

ON THAT SEPTEMBER summer evening, as the sun began to set, an acoustic guitarist played "Over the Rainbow." I tried to breathe it all in: the flutters in my stomach, the scene in front of me, the fairy tale of it all. Jonathan was between us, in his little blue collared shirt and tan suit, holding our hands as he walked us down the aisle. I looked around at our guests—family and friends who gave us the gift of their presence, support, and love.

Then, out of the corner of my eye, I saw my father.

Though we were estranged, I had invited my father out of obligation, pressured by my grandparents and not out of any true desire to have him there. I'd not spoken to him on a regular basis for years, so I was shocked when we received his reply card. And now here he was, three rows in, watching me get married to a woman he never even knew I loved.

A handful of memories came to mind in that moment: those gifts he'd sent instead of being present, him calling me "spoiled" in a letter he sent to my grandma when I was eight years old. My gaze lingered a little longer in his direction, and then I stuffed down my sadness, trying to replace it with the day's happiness.

We took our places, Jonathan, Dinushka, and I, standing in front as the song came to an end. The priest's words broke through the silence.

"We have come together in the presence of God to witness and bless the covenant of love and fidelity which Dinushka and Nikkya have made to each other."

Our community stood with us as we exchanged vows with each other, and then with Jonathan. We stood together before him, opened a box with a white gold cross inside, and said, "We, your moms, vow to love you, support you, and be with you always for the rest of our lives, with God's hand guiding us all." He put his hands on both sides of his face, happily squishing his cheeks, and then opened his arms to receive our hugs.

Before the ceremony concluded, we offered the Eucharist in honor of my mother, a sacrament celebrating the sacrifice of Jesus. I asked Poppy, the man I considered to be my father, to help the priest pass out the bread and wine. After I ate and drank, I watched Poppy quietly, admiring how my grandfather took pride in offering the sacrament to people he'd never met before. He was doing God's work on my special day.

Our ceremony concluded with a short kiss, both of us careful not to offend our religious aunts and uncles. We made our way back up the stairs to cheers celebrating our love and then moved into the reception hall, which was filled with the flowers I'd picked out all those months before. Arrangements of light and deep purple, blue and white, were planted in rustic logs, atop lavender tablecloths. Each guest received a Dilmah tea bag from Dinushka's homeland and a small square piece of love cake, another special Sri Lankan treat. We had a candy bar, with all my favorites, from Twizzlers to taffy, and small bags with our initials on the front for guests to fill up.

"At Last" by Etta James played as we invited everyone to dance our first dance with us. The music transitioned to Stevie Wonder, Michael Jackson, and M.I.A., and Dinushka and I snuck away, followed by her mother and her mother's best friends, who all helped us dress in our sarees. Mine was pink and gold, while Dinushka's—which had belonged to her grandmother—was blue, red, and gold. The tightly wrapped robes hugged our bodies perfectly as we returned to the dance floor in our new outfits, just in time to join a Soul Train Line led by my brother Danny.

The DJ then transitioned to Bollywood songs, and my heart melted as I saw my grandmother dancing with my uncle Bob, both smiling from ear to ear while trying to keep in step with the new South Asian dance they were learning. Our reception ended with a lively and crowded dance floor made up of both of our families and our friends, old and young, Muslims, Hindus, Christians, and atheists, all dancing side by side in the name of love.

MY GRANDPARENTS WATCHED Jonathan at our apartment while Dinushka and I went to Key West on our honeymoon. We spent countless hours just walking and talking, getting to know each other all over again. It was the most time we had had alone together since we'd brought Jonathan back from his stay in Virginia three and a half years ago. In Key West, we were free to hold hands without stares from straight people. Being together in all our gay glory was unlocking dormant emotions, dusting them off, and letting them go. We were just us—affectionate and in love for all to see.

When we got home, my grandparents seemed happy to not only have had the time with Jonathan but also to have been able to give us the gift of childcare so we could get away. They could not help pay for our wedding, but they could give us this. Almost as soon as we stepped into our apartment, they provided a run-down of what had happened while we were gone.

"The chicken from your wedding was so good. We've been eating leftovers all week," my grandfather told us.

"Dinushka's parents stopped by, and we chatted for a while," Nanny added. "It was such a good wedding. D's family knows how to have a good time."

The next time Dinushka and I saw her parents, they let us know that they'd found my grandparents so down-to-earth. "They are good people," her father added warmly. He was happy to see everyone get along. "Nikkya looked beautiful in saree," he gushed before he went on to talk more about Nanny and Poppy.

These conversations revealed what I'd long hoped we would develop between our families: kinship. I wondered if I'd ever feel this way about Karl, if I would ever come to see the good in him amidst the dysfunction. I knew those feelings would be hard won if I ever found them at all.

20

I'D WORKED SO hard to have a different life than the one I knew growing up, but we were still, after all these years, schlepping to and from Long Island to satisfy an irresponsible, self-serving man's desire to say "I am his father" and then not act like a father. Dinushka and I couldn't live freely like any other couple, couldn't be secure in knowing that Jonathan was ours forever, even though we were now married. It was an exhausting state to be in—always on edge about what request may or may not come from Karl—and feeling like we *had* to always say yes, lest there be some kind of retaliation. For most of Jonathan's early childhood, I waded in ever-present terror that he could be taken from us at any time.

But then again, I feared just about everything when it came to taking on the role of Jonathan's mother—even the very fact that he called me Mommy made me worry about how that might impact him later in life.

JONATHAN HAD A natural curiosity about how things worked and why they worked in a particular way. He loved nature and hikes, picked up worms in the mud, and asked why they were so wiggly. At our local nature center, he wanted to touch all the animals. His normally overactive self would calm down while holding a snake or petting a goat.

Jonathan sang the songs he learned in school and asked me to record them on my phone. I would chuckle and clap after a performance of "Twinkle, Twinkle, Little Star." It was a joy watching his personality bloom, but it was also difficult to see developmental and behavioral issues persist. He still struggled to maintain eye contact with strangers and family alike.

Dinnertime became a battle, as he would only eat pasta or rice. Sometimes, minutes after eating, he would throw up, or flail on the floor over some vegetable or new meat we had introduced. The minor sensory issues he'd had in the past grew worse.

I found that I became quick to anger, snapping back at Dinushka when she said Jonathan's behavior wasn't typical— even though I knew she was not wrong. I was trying to convince myself that his toddler spirit just wanted to be able to control something when there was so much in his life beyond his control. I couldn't figure out how to connect with these behaviors that I'd never known in a child before. A part of me harbored anger toward Dinushka, because she seemed to understand him every single step of the way—and always have the answers. I was failing to come up with any at all.

We started using rewards as encouragement, remembering

that Jonathan, now six, loved it when his new first-grade teacher offered him something from her treasure box if he opened doors for people, cleaned up after play, or turned his classwork in on time. Ms. Roth gave him the positive attention he craved, especially after being labeled the "bad kid" in preschool.

At the end of his first-grade year, we asked the school for an academic and psychological evaluation and were denied. We were told that academically he was doing well and there was no cause to worry even if socially he was struggling.

Since the school did not want to pay the hefty price tag to evaluate him, it was now our job to find a neuropsychologist. It wasn't until he turned seven that he was officially diagnosed with an autism spectrum and adjustment disorder with anxiety—so many words and labels I was still ill prepared for.

DINUSHKA WAS INVOLVED, as many parents would be, in Jonathan's academics. As a former elementary and middle school teacher, she began creating checklists with pictures, like an image of a boy brushing his teeth to encourage Jonathan to do the same. If he followed through on his chores for the day, he'd get his favorite food—doughnuts.

Dinushka was listed as an emergency contact, and the school finally began to recognize her as one of his parents. On every form, we crossed out *father* and wrote in *mother*, and at every school meeting, we explained our family dynamic as a "two-mom household." It felt like we were coming out over and over again.

"The school sees the three of us as family because we are

one," Dinushka told Jonathan on the drive home one day. "Like Mommy, I take care of you and love you. I am one of your parents, but instead of a dad, I am your other mom."

As we waited at the stoplight, I turned around to look at him, trying to gauge his reaction. He appeared to be deep in thought, perhaps curious if we were waiting for a response from him or not. He broke his gaze from staring out of the window and looked at Dinushka and then me.

"We are a family," he said.

I wanted my son to feel secure about his place in my life. He had me *and* Dinushka, two women—two moms—who were going to fight for him. As a child, my grandmother had told me that I could not call her Mom, and I understood her reasons, but it was my grandmother, not my mother, who endured sleepless nights when I was an infant, who held me when I had coughs and sniffles and fevers. She was the one who taught me how to be a mother—through the laughs we shared, the lessons she imparted about respecting others and believing in my own capabilities. She taught me about independence and how to support myself, instilling in me a fierce sense that I was resilient.

Nanny also modeled for me how to care for a family by the unconditional love she gave to her own daughter, my mother. But I was realizing more and more that we'd never had the hard conversations. I rarely saw my grandparents argue or disagree. We never sat down to explore why my mother became a drug addict or why my uncle Wayne started to drink at the age of nine. This lack of communication was not something I wanted to continue in the family Dinushka and I had built.

THE YEAR AFTER our wedding, at the end of spring, I got the call that Poppy had been in an accident. My grandfather had spent the morning picking up recyclables, tending to his customers, and being his usual dependable self when the worst happened.

At 9:45 a.m., at the border of Amelia and Chesterfield Counties in Central Virginia, Poppy crossed an intersection on a busy country road and hit an uprooted tree. The airbag never deployed, and Poppy was thrown from the truck. Medics airlifted his body to VCU Medical Center in Richmond.

I called Dinushka at work and told her what had happened. I needed to get to Virginia right away.

"Pack your black dress," she said.

Fifteen minutes later, we both left our offices in New York City to race home to Connecticut to pack and pick up Jonathan. Later, Dinushka would tell me she had quickly dipped into church and prayed for Poppy: *If there is life in him give him life, Lord. If there is life in him give him life, Lord. If there is life in him give him life, Lord.* After her prayer, thunder rumbled and lightning flashed. A bad storm was raging, and her heart sank in dread. She wept on the altar steps.

Dinushka and I drove seven and a half hours, straight to the hospital, to meet my family in the waiting area of the ICU. By the time we arrived, my grandfather had already undergone two emergency surgeries to remove his spleen and stop the internal bleeding. Both of his lungs were punctured, and he had brain damage.

Before we were allowed to see him, a chaplain took immediate family members to a conference room to update us and prepare us. By Virginia state law, if the neurological tests they were performing came back showing he had no brain activity, he would be declared legally dead. We would need to decide as a family how long we would want to keep him on the ventilator, if we were told that he would never recover.

"We will wait to make any official decisions. His kids are on their way, and I want them to see him," my grandmother said, staring down at the table. "But I know my husband would not want to be kept alive if he were brain-dead."

My heart ached for her—for us all. I prayed that by some miracle Poppy would wake up and open his eyes. That he would get out of his bed and walk. He never wanted to live a life where he couldn't do for himself—for him, that was not living. Sitting by his bedside, I looked through his overstuffed black wallet, at the pictures of everyone he carried with him. There were four photos of me, every one of them peeling and faded, a telltale sign that he'd carried them around for a long, long time. There was me as a scrawny toddler with a wide smile and big teeth, as a child in a knitted purple-and-pink sweater, as a smooth, cool teenager with greasy hair and hope in my eyes. Then my college self, wearing my cap and gown, proof that our hard work had paid off. He'd kept them all, just like a father would for his daughter.

I held his soft, swollen hand, the hand of a man who had been holding mine for my entire life. "Your only job, Pop, is to get better," I whispered.

I told him that I would take care of him and be there for him for whatever he needed. I told him that Jonathan asked what a miracle was and if a miracle would happen to him. I read him a scripture from Psalms.

The Lord is my shepherd, I shall not want.
He makes me lie down in green pastures.
He leads me beside still waters.
He restores my soul.
He leads me in paths of righteousness
for his name's sake.
Even though I walk through the valley of the shadow of
death,
I will fear no evil,
for you are with me;
your rod and your staff, they comfort me.

I knew it was silly of me, but I thought telling him that his work was not done on Earth would make him come back to life. I told Poppy that I loved him. But as I let go of his hands, I knew he had left this earth. I felt God was there with us in that room.

After the doctors performed their final test, they gathered us again and said that, despite all their efforts, the results revealed that there was no brain activity. Poppy was pronounced dead.

We all piled into his room—five of his children, twelve of his grandchildren, sons- and daughters-in-law, the chaplain, his nurses, and the organ donation staff—surrounding his bed. I began to sing "This Little Light of Mine," and the others followed.

As we sang and cried, the clouds parted and sunlight filled the room.

21

AFTER POPPY'S DEATH, we were fragile and raw—our tanks were empty; we'd hit a wall. Yet eventually, the loss also lit a fire in us. It helped Dinushka and me find a confidence we'd not had before. We knew we had to stop living in fear that our son would be taken away from us. We were Jonathan's parents in every single way except on paper. We needed to legally adopt him.

Though we were in Connecticut and married, we still felt we had to drive to Long Island to visit Karl. While the frequency of requests for visits had lessened, along with Karl's interest in spending time with Jonathan, we continued to shuffle him back and forth, wasting gas to stroke the ego of a man who loved himself more than his biological son.

Dinushka and I had pushed ourselves professionally to secure a better life for life for our family. Dinushka was by now a pediatric chaplain in a hospital and clergy in the Episcopal Church. I wrote and also worked for a nonprofit, helping people who looked like me and were facing financial struggles with health care costs. For eight years, I'd been too afraid to ask Karl a simple question: Can I adopt Jonathan? I'd been worried about what his answer would be, worried the question itself would send him into an emotional tailspin that would land us all back in family court. But I had let fear rule our lives for far too long.

"Just do it," Dinushka encouraged me. "What can he say? No? But what if he says yes—then we're free."

I knew rationally there would never be a "right time" to ask a man to willingly terminate his parental rights, but serendipitously, Karl called, letting me know he was feeling frustrated by the child support the courts were demanding of him. He didn't want to pay but would go to jail if he failed to do so.

"Karl, there's something I've been thinking a lot about. I know you know that I am trying to do right for Jonathan. You agreed to allow us to move to Connecticut. Would you agree to allow me to adopt him? The adoption would end your concerns about child support."

"Sure," he said, as if he'd been waiting for the question for years, relieved he didn't have to make payments anymore.

"I'll need to figure out what that really means for us to go ahead with it. Can I call you back later this week once I know more?"

"Yeah, that'll work," he said.

And that was that.

KARL WOULD FIRST need to sign over his rights—under Connecticut law, this was called a voluntary termination. We wouldn't need to go in front of a judge for this part of the process, but instead a legal document could be picked up from the courthouse in Connecticut and then signed by Karl in New York or in Connecticut, as long as it was notarized. I was panicked that Karl would go back on his word, so I hurried to get the papers together. Two weeks after that initial phone conversation, Jonathan and I sat in Karl's gravel driveway, waiting for him to take his seat on the passenger side. The papers were neatly folded in a business-sized white envelope in my door.

It wasn't logical, but I'd decided to bring Jonathan with me that day because even though I was tempting fate, I couldn't resist seeing if Karl might want to fight for his own son. But it didn't happen. Karl got into the car and gave us both a happier hello than he'd given us in years. We drove to a bank to have the documents notarized. A man dressed in a dark suit welcomed us and sat us down. He looked over the piece of paper I handed him and asked if we both understood it. We nodded, and Karl signed. Then out came the heavy silver notary tool, sealing our new fates.

"Well, shall we go get lunch?" I asked.

TWO MONTHS LATER, after two home visits from the Connecticut Department of Children and Families, we had a date for our adoption proceeding. It was just weeks before we were set to move into a new home. Our social worker wasn't at all concerned that we were two moms, and he'd made a real effort to get to know us. Each time he came to visit, he looked at the framed photo collage of Jonathan—a gift from Lauren—on the wall. We hoped he saw in those pictures Jonathan's joy and the stable life he had. The social worker assured us that since we had our adoption court date set, we had nothing to fear. We had his blessing.

We began boxing up our belongings, scheduling the moving truck, and ordering new furniture—preparing for moving day. It had taken Dinushka a long time to be ready to assume the responsibilities of homeownership: paying the mortgage, mowing the grass, fixing anything that needed fixing. I knew Dinushka had also been hesitant to buy a house because it would be another change for us. She didn't like change.

So we went slowly. First, we set the parameters for the location. Then we decided on what we wanted in a house and gave our list to her father, who helped us along the way and then answered our many questions when we agreed on a house: Can we ask the seller to leave the fridge? Can we ask the seller to paint? What does this mean in the inspection report?

For Dinushka, this house was a new stage that she'd need to get used to. For me, this house was an opportunity, a place we could put down roots and grow our family. It gave me a sense of normalcy.

The house, with green aluminum siding, was built in 1927. It was one of the first built on the block. With a shed that was once a horse stable, a basement that was once used to brew beer, the previous owners, a family of seven, had raised their five daughters in the two-bedroom home that we were now the owners of. There were hardwood floors throughout, and a sunporch I could see myself writing in. When we walked in, it felt like home for both of us. It was perfect for the three of us and our little Australian terrier named Lucky.

Not yet unpacked, we went to the adoption proceeding in June 2014. We all sat nervously in the small reception area, waiting for our names to be called. Jonathan, now eight years old and wearing his best polo shirt and khaki pants, looked up at us and asked, "I will be a Hargrove De Silva now?"

Dinushka smiled widely and nodded. Perhaps Jonathan didn't understand all the details of what was happening, but he was as happy as we were.

The secretary came out to tell us that the judge was finishing up another case, and we'd be next. Her smile offered an apology for the delay that made me feel like we would finally be taken seriously by the same system that had forced us into the agreement with Karl all those years ago. I had dreamed of this day for a long time and imagined I'd feel this way if I ever gave birth to my own child—full of elation, apprehension, urgency, and an unwavering desire to give my child the best shot in life they could have.

When it was our turn, we entered a warm and inviting office. Dinushka, Jonathan, and I fumbled while we each chose one of the antique-looking seats, shuffling around a large table as if we were playing a game of musical chairs. When we were settled, the judge looked at Jonathan, who was sitting at the head of the table.

"Do you know why we are here?"

"I think so," Jonathan answered. "To change my last name and make our family official."

"Do you agree with what is about to happen, how your family is about to change?"

"Yes," he said.

"Do you take these two people as your moms?"

"Yes," he said.

And then it was our turn.

"Do you accept the responsibility you are about to forever commit to?"

"Yes," Dinushka and I said in unison.

"Do you understand the importance of today?"

"Yes," Dinushka and I said in unison.

"And there you have it, young man. You are adopted!"

The judge confirmed the adoption with one smash of his gavel, and Jonathan smiled ear to ear, knowing that his new name would be Jonathan Hargrove De Silva.

Jonathan was ours, and we were his. We hugged our caseworker, snapped a family photo with the judge, and then went out to celebrate at Dinushka's parents'—now officially Jonathan's grandparents'—house. Together, we danced and danced, happily laughing with relief. We were a family—in deed, in action, and, as always, in love.

Epilogue

SAYING THE WORDS *I love you* to a child you are no longer afraid of losing is liberating.

Today, we are a family of five, with a son, twin daughters, and two moms. My mother never got the chance to experience the kind of love that I get to experience with my family every single day, and I am forever grateful for this gift it took me so long to believe I was worthy of.

There is only one photo I've ever found of my mother holding me as an infant. It's faded from the years it's been stuck in an album at my grandmother's house, an album that came along with us every time we moved. In the photo, my mother is lying down in bed and I am asleep on her chest. Her eyes are closed and her lips gently pressed against my forehead. I've now done the same thing with all three of my children—still in the moment, connecting in an unspoken way that seals us as one.

For twenty-five years, I waited for my mother to show me the kind of love depicted in that photo—in action and not just in word. I waited all those years for her to become someone she never could. My mother's legacy isn't simply her mistakes or her faults, but that she did not have the faith or courage to believe in herself or to believe that those kinds of dreams could actually be her reality.

It saddens me now to know that she never knew love the way I know love, the way I give love, the way I am loved by Dinushka. There aren't words to describe how my wife looks at me, believes in me, and gives of herself to me, how she defines family for me. It saddens me that my mother never looked at her kids and knew they felt safe and protected by every decision she made, the way my kids know that every day.

WHEN I WAS young, I held my breath every single time my teachers or my friends brought up the word *family*. How would I explain my situation? I carried so much shame about my father's absence and my mother's addiction and about being raised by my grandparents. If I had talked with those friends or teachers, maybe I would have learned that many families have problems, and that I was okay. I'm grateful to have had Nanny and Poppy to fill my biological parents' shoes.

I'm still trying not to be my mother. Until Jonathan came into my life, I didn't make the attempt to revisit those wounds from childhood, but we must all reckon with our past at some point. Now I go to therapy and try to unpack what has happened, try to manage the symptoms of what I now know is complex post-traumatic stress disorder (CPTSD), a diagnosis that didn't come until I was thirty-seven years old.

The word *trauma* wasn't used in the home I grew up in, but it makes sense given that I have a hard time trusting people, that my memory isn't that great, and that in order to get through those hard days I had to bury all the painful parts. As a child, I'd wanted the one person who could not give me all of herself—my mother. Growing up, I ended up protecting myself from that reality the only way I knew how: by building walls around my emotions, locking them away in an effort to keep myself safe. I was not beaten or abused, but I now know I was neglected.

The moment I decided I wanted to be a mother—Jonathan's mother—was the moment I decided to not let that trauma affect my own kids. Some call it hope, some call it determination, but whatever it was, I held tightly to it, knowing, seeing, and feeling the kind of life I envisioned for myself and my kids. I never want my children to feel the kind of shame I did, to hold on to the kind of secrets I held. I know it's not their job to protect me like I protected my mother.

Jonathan has taught me how to stay the course, to not allow my dreams or demons to steer me away from being his mother. I don't run when things get difficult. And with Dinushka's help, I am able to pause when I need to and then move ahead with decisions that are best for our family. I've learned to listen to her insight about our kids.

Our kids don't worry about whether or not someone will show up for their soccer game. They don't worry about whether they will get to celebrate holidays like Christmas or Halloween with their parents. And most of all, they never have to wonder about if we are a family or their place in it.

As I write this, Jonathan's seventeenth birthday is approaching and I am not ready. Time has gone by so fast and yet so slow, and we have weathered many storms, but when asked why he has two moms, or where his dad is, Jonathan can answer with confidence. There are times when he needs to teach others—about inclusivity, about queerness, about nontraditional families. Just as heterosexual moms of color must arm their kids with appropriate responses to all the questions and microaggressions that come their way, Dinushka and I, as queer parents, must do the same.

I know that Jonathan and his sisters will find flaws in how they were parented—of course they will—but I also know that they are proud and secure. Dinushka and I have tried to show our kids that something will always bowl you over, but you have the strength to get up again, that there is power in forgiveness and in hard work. Every person, no matter their place in the world, deserves the comfort of knowing that whatever struggles they face, they do not face them alone.

We have made a home full of love, with photos of so many family memories lining our walls, side by side with our kids' artwork. We randomly leave sticky notes for each other—on the television, on walls, on bathroom mirrors—saying things like "I love you very much" and "Have a wonderful day. You are the best."

Each year, nearing Christmas, we fill backpacks or gift bags for the unhoused, which our kids pass out on street corners. I still remember a small village we came across one year. The men living there had formed a community by building huts from scraps of wood from a local carpentry store. They had also built a ladder that led into the trees, along with several birdhouses. Birds of varied colors surrounded them, wings flapping above like small angels.

Home is where there is life and love. And as I saw my children look around and up in this small village, I felt immense gratitude.

With my family, I am no longer lost. I am found.

Acknowledgments

I'D LIKE TO thank my family for always supporting me in the best way they know how. Thank you, especially to Natasha, Main, Kendra, Lady, She-She, and Wayne. I am forever grateful for Nanny, Poppy, and my mother, Lisa, who gave me the best parts of who they were. To Poppy, who always told me I'd "be a writer"—here, I am, Poppy, and thank you for believing in me. To Aunty, Uncle, Sanjit, Deepa, and Ishan, thank you for loving and embracing me, for believing in me, and for welcoming me into your family.

A heartfelt thank-you to my agent, Stacey Glick, for believing in my words and for walking with me every step of the way; to my editor, Amy Gash, for reminding me that there is certainly more to say, and for your ability to push me a little further; to Stacey May Fowles, for the generosity of your time, compassion, and keen sense of storytelling. Thank you to Lindsay Wolf and Jen Cummings for reading and for your thoughtful feedback along the way.

Thank you also to the people who supported me even before the book was born. To those who helped in so many ways, from picking up my kids so I could write, to sending texts reminding me to keep going, and for giving me an opportunity to simply talk about "this book": Diana Saguilan, Lauren Pessin, Betsaida Alcantara, Zac Decker, Cara Parks, Sarah Halpern, Liz Howort, Joseph Belisle, David Vintinner, Emily Steinberg, Sonya Huber, and Diana Lee. A shout-out to the (many) wonderful coffee shops I spent time in for the conversations, the atmosphere, and the copious amounts of coffee—The Corner, Frenchies Coffee Bar, Open Door Tea, and Walnut Beach Coffee House—thank you for keeping me caffeinated!

There aren't enough words to adequately thank Dinushka De Silva for reading and rereading and editing, and for telling me the truth about the words that just didn't fit. Thank you for being a part of my story, for allowing me to borrow your memory, and for believing in me even when I did not. But most of all, thank you for loving me and for building this family with me.

To Oliver and Evelyn, thank you for helping to distract me with your need for walks, treats, and doggie playtime. To Aviah De Silva and Lera De Silva—thank you for your patience, your honesty, and your reminders that I can take a break from writing to play with you! And with all my heart and all of my love, thank you to Jonathan De Silva for being the one I call my son—I love you.